The Definitive Guide to Criminal Justice and Criminology on the World Wide Web

Second Edition

Frank Schmalleger, Ph.D.
Director, The Justice Research Association
and Professor Emeritus,
The University of North Carolina at Pembroke

Prentice
Hall

Prentice Hall, Upper Saddle River, New Jersey 07458

Library of Congress Cataloging-in-Publication Data

The definitive guide to criminal justice and criminology on the World Wide Web/Frank
Schmalleger [director]; foreword by Cecil E. Greek.—2nd ed.
    p. cm.
  Includes bibliographical references and index.
  ISBN 0-13-091590-4
    1. Criminal justice, Administration of—United States—Computer network resources. 2.
  Criminal justice, Administration of—United states—Computer network
  resources—Directories. 3. Criminology—United States—Computer network resources. 4.
  Criminology—United States—Computer network resources—Directories. I. Schmalleger,
  Frank.

KF242.C72 D44 2002
025.06'364—dc21   2001034376

Publisher: Jeff Johnston
Executive Assistant: Brenda Rock
Executive Acquisitions Editor: Kim Davies
Assistant Editor: Sarah Holle
Managing Editor: Mary Carnis
Production Liaison: Adele M. Kupchik
Production Editor: Janet Bolton
**Director of Manufacturing
    and Production:** Bruce Johnson
Manufacturing Manger: Ilene Sanford
Manufacturing Buyer: Cathleen Petersen

Creative Director: Cheryl Asherman
Senior Design Coordinator: Miguel Ortiz
Cover Design: Joseph Sengotta
Cover Art: Cameron Beck, SIS/Images.com
Interior Design/Composition: Janet Bolton
Electronic Art Creation: Mark Ammerman
Marketing Manager: Ramona Sherman
Printing and Binding: R.R. Donnelley and Sons,
    Crawfordsville
Proofreader: Maine Proofreading Services
Copy Editor: Judy Coughlin

Pearson Education LTD.
Pearson Education Australia PTY, Limited
Pearson Education Singapore, Pte. Ltd.
Pearson Education North Asia Ltd.
Pearson Education Canada, Ltd.
Pearson Educacion de Mexico, S.A. de C.V.
Pearson Education—Japan
Pearson Education Malaysia, Pte. Ltd.

10 9 8 7 6 5 4 3 2 1
ISBN 0-13-091590-4

Contents

4   E-Mail and E-Mail Software   59

5   E-Mail Discussion Lists, Newsgroups, 'Zines, and E-Journals   73

6   Search Engines and Web Maps   89

7   Netiquette and Web Manners   105

8   Criminal Justice Careers Online   117

9   Security Issues   131

10   Using the *Talk Justice* Site   145

Foreword

The best aspect of the Internet has nothing to do with technology. It's us. Getting in touch with each other is more exciting than the coolest computer game or the hottest information.

—*Newsweek Magazine*
(via America Online's Talking E-Mail service, January 5, 1998)

Those who use the Internet daily can probably remember the moment they first discovered its truly universal value. For me it was a day in 1994, when a copy of Mosaic was placed on my newly networked office computer. Discovering that one could find materials easily and design one's own multimedia-filled Web pages was life-changing for me.

Like many others who have found the Internet an indispensable tool in their everyday lives, it's swiftly becoming more and more difficult for me to remember what things were like before it. If, for example, I had to revert to teaching my criminology courses without Web pages, discussion forums, and e-mail, I'd probably look for another endeavor.

Discussions of the Internet and the World Wide Web now take place everywhere: in classrooms, on campus, in newspapers, and on television. While the criminal justice community was a little late in catching the wave, it's now quickly making up for lost time. At the 1998 Academy of Criminal Justice Sciences meetings in Albuquerque, New Mexico, there were over 100 papers on various topics related to the Internet and distance learning. It is to these discussions, and how they are impacting criminology and the criminal justice field, that this book contributes. While many have become expert users of the Internet, new faculty, students, and practitioners get online for the first time every day. Others find that once the initial euphoria wears off, it's difficult to locate the right information quickly—particularly high-quality criminal-justice-related information.

This text serves as a major road map for criminal justice Net users. Designed specifically to look at the Internet from a criminal-justice-centered perspective, the book offers something for beginners and for intermediate and advanced users. For example, the material on e-mail starts with the basics, moves on to discussions of Net e-mail etiquette (netiquette) and ethics, and ends with examples of the growing number of e-mail-based discussion lists available to the criminal justice community. If you're looking for technical assistance, such as how to unsubscribe from a mailing list, it's here. However, the focus remains on the value of mailing lists for those in criminal justice.

There are many useful indices in the book, each presenting a number of Web sites to which the reader can refer for additional information on criminal justice on the Net. Particularly useful is the chapter on criminal justice careers online (Chapter 8). It might even slow the e-mail flow to folks like me, from students asking, "What can I do with a degree in criminology?" or "Where can I find criminal justice jobs?"

Another hot topic—and one with which this book deals—is security. Those working in criminal justice need to pay special attention to Net security issues. From making sure that e-mail is not inadvertently captured by the wrong person(s) to protecting the network infrastructure on which our business, governmental, and military institutions now are built, security is a major concern. As dramatic as is the current need for information technology experts, those trained in computer crime prevention, computer forensics, and network security already are much in demand.

It appears that the Web is now poised to become a major vehicle for criminal justice distance learning, virtual collaboration, and intrasystem communication. A brief note on each follows.

By combining the software talents of those producing online gaming worlds, 3D virtual spaces, and avatars with text and voice chat environments, we predict that interactive simulations will become a major form of criminal justice distance learning. Students as avatars will participate not only in simulated 3D classrooms, but will work through scenarios as varied as crime scene investigations, courtroom procedures, and jail and prison management. In such a learning environment, Web pages, on-line databases, newsgroups, and clip art galleries can be employed to prepare students to be better role players and, ultimately perhaps, more effective police officers, attorneys, and citizens.

Virtual collaboration will blossom as the Web provides inexpensive real-time access for group endeavors. Collaboration software (e.g., Microsoft NetMeeting®) already permits shared text and audio chat, embedded Web cams, exchange of files, a shared white board, group demos through sharing programs over a network, and group work on a single copy of a software program (e.g., a desktop publishing program). As the ability to translate text into the readers' languages on the fly becomes more efficient, global communication will increase dramatically. Virtual collaboration will allow distant researchers to carry out their projects, law enforcement agencies to securely exchange sensitive case information, and students to work with faculty and experts of their choosing.

Communication between the various branches of the criminal justice system is now much easier. An example comes from the police department of Largo, Florida, and their efforts to provide instant information on domestic violence cases to the courts and victims' shelters. Officers take photographs and record audio at the crime scene. By 10 A.M. the next morning, a digital case file is created in the form of a Web page with photos, 911 tapes, and scanned reports. The judge handling the initial appearance to set bail has access to the Web pages, and, for the first time, can make truly informed decisions. Local victims' shelters are given password access to the Web sites as well, and are thus able to determine the seriousness of the woman's injuries and possible need for intervention.

These measures, combined with other domestic violence model policies, have led to a nearly 100 percent guilty plea rate for Largo arrestees. Efforts such as these will continue to sprout up. In the not too distant future, we envision officers in squad cars equipped with laptops and wireless modems browsing to secure Web forms to fill out their reports and sending the reports instantly into a database server, resulting in immediately available case information for those who need access.

The first step in making use of these hybrid networked technologies is a good understanding of the Internet's basic protocols, such as e-mail, the Web, newsgroups, FTP, and chat. It is our hope that this text will unleash for you the potential that the Internet has for criminology and criminal justice.

Cecil E. Greek
Associate Professor of Criminology, Florida State University
Co-Director, The Criminal Justice Distance Learning Consortium

Preface

I do not fear computers. I fear the lack of them.

—Isaac Asimov

As we move through the first decade of the twenty-first century, the future of criminal justice education confronts us. It has become clear to many of us in the justice field that education within our discipline is increasingly embracing the distance learning model. Look around, and you will see that the call for quality distance education is being taken up by an ever-growing cadre of students, educators, and professionals. That call is being met by an increase in the number of distance learning programs—at both the graduate and undergraduate level—that are now being offered.

Much of what is possible in the field of distance learning builds substantially on the World Wide Web. The Web, which is barely a decade old, holds the potential to extensively alter the way in which the educational enterprise is conducted.

With this trend in mind, I am proud to welcome you to the second edition of *The Definitive Guide to Criminal Justice and Criminology on the World Wide Web*. This guide is supported by a dedicated Web site that you can reach at http://talkjustice.com. Both the guide and the Web site are sponsored by my agency, the Justice Research Association (JRA), the Criminal Justice Distance Learning Consortium (CJDLC), and Prentice Hall Publishing Company.

In assembling this guide, we here at JRA and CJDLC wanted to make available a comprehensive print volume that students in the disciplines of criminal justice and criminology could use to learn about the fantastic resources offered by the World Wide Web. We also wanted to develop a justice-specific guide—not merely a book built around a general framework with criminal justice and criminology content added as an afterthought (as some guides do). I hope you will agree that we have succeeded on both counts.

As you read through this guide you will learn about the historical development of the Internet and the Web. If you don't already know how to surf the Web, or are hesitant about your skill level, you will be introduced to the software, hardware, and types of connections needed to enter today's world of Internet technology. E-mail, Web search engines, security issues, netiquette (Web etiquette), and careers in criminal justice and criminology are all discussed.

Among the most useful features of this guide, however, are the up-to-date and comprehensive lists of Web resources that it contains. Chapter 3, for example, lists dozens of useful criminology and criminal justice sites on the Web. Chapter 8 provides a catalog of career resources available via the Internet and includes links to many government and private job sites. An Internet glossary, provided by SquareOne Technology, follows the chapters and rounds out this volume.

The *Talk Justice* site is discussed in the final chapter. It supports this guide in a number of ways. First, the site is built around a discussion group feature, making it possible for visitors to leave messages for other site participants, to thread those messages, and to reenter the ongoing discussion at any time. A chat facility makes it possible for our guests to participate in real-time discussions with others about any criminal justice-related issue. The *Talk Justice* Cybrary, one of the site's central features, contains all of the links listed in this guide—and more. Constant updating of the Cybrary ensures that links are as current as possible. Should you come across a link in this guide that is dated or no longer functions, please visit the Cybrary for updated link information.

We also invite you to visit the Justice Research Association. Point your Web browser at http://cjcentral.com/jra and you will reach the JRA home page. There you will find a description of our activities, including a discussion of our role in creating and maintaining this guide and a description of ongoing efforts to build our most comprehensive project to date—the Criminal Justice Distance Learning Consortium (CJDLC). You can visit the CJDLC at http://cjcentral.com/cjdlc.

Enjoy the guide. Should you have any comments or suggestions for improvement, please send them to me at admin@talkjustice.com.

ACKNOWLEDGMENTS

The author would like to thank the following for their assistance in developing this guide: Dr. Charles Ousley, Seminole State College; Tere Chipman, Fayetteville Technical Community College; and Harry Babb, SUNY—Famingdale.

Frank Schmalleger, Ph.D.
Professor Emeritus, The University of North Carolina at Pembroke
Founder & Co-Director, The Criminal Justice Distance Learning Consortium

The publisher and the author of this book jointly donate a portion of sales proceeds to research and education in the field of crime and justice.

1

A Brief History of the Internet

What hath God wrought?

—*Samuel F. B. Morse, in the first telegraph message ever sent (1844)*

If you want to stay current...into the [twenty-first] century, you need to learn about the Internet. Futurists predict that information and access to it will be the basis for personal, business, and political advancement in the [twenty-first] century....The Internet can shrink the world and bring knowledge, experience, and information on nearly every subject imaginable straight to your computer.

—*The Electronic Frontier Foundation's Guide to the Internet*[1]

CHAPTER OUTLINE

WHAT IS THE INTERNET?

The Internet is a vast collection of computers tied together by an electronic network that spans the globe. The Internet, a late-twentieth-century creation, has had a significant impact on how people communicate. Its influence is growing exponentially and will be felt well into the twenty-first century and beyond.

The Internet is bringing about a qualitative change in the way people live, work, and learn. As a consequence, it ranks among the greatest inventions of all time.

Some people compare the development of the Internet to the invention of the printing press—which in its early days as a hand-powered machine dramatically changed communications. The widespread and relatively easy distribution of thoughts and ideas through the medium of print (such as books, newspapers, and magazines) shaped a number of vitally important events over the course of centuries, including wars, political campaigns, revolutions, and the growth of scientific knowledge.

Internet: a vast collection of computers tied together by an electronic network that spans the globe.

As Michael Hanrahan explains, "Much like the Gutenberg Press radically changed the way people communicated in 16th Century Europe, the Internet is in the process of revolutionizing our communication, information distribution, and the very structure of our lives."[2] Some contemporary social commentators put it this way:

The information age has been ushered in by new and powerful methods of communication. Gutenberg's invention of the printing press took books out of the ecclesiastical libraries and put them into the hands of the people. Then, the telephone system emerged to allow people instantaneous communication with one another. Now the Internet merges both these technologies, bringing people and information together without the middleman (publisher) necessitated by books or the primarily one-to-one synchronous limitations of the telephone system. This is a new dimension—an electronic, virtual world where time and space have almost no meaning. People in geographically distant lands communicate across time zones without ever seeing each other, and information is available 24 hours a day from thousands of places. The implications of this new global communication and information system are staggering.[3]

The Internet is a child of the information age—an era characterized by rapid communication and the electronic dissemination of information. The information age has a relatively long history, going back at least 140 years. Some people[4] trace the beginning of the modern age of information to 1858—the year that the first transatlantic telegraph cable was laid. That cable attempted to provide instantaneous communication between Europe and the North American continent. Although the cable remained in service for only a few days before succumbing to the turbulent waters of the North Atlantic, the technology it represented provided a quantum leap beyond the slow physical transmission of information required by the printing press. In 1866 a new and successful transatlantic cable was laid, and it remained in use for almost a century.

The historical event that was to have the most immediate impact on the development of the Internet, however, was the October 1957 launching of the world's first artificial satellite. Named *Sputnik 1*, the 10-pound device was sent into orbit by the former Soviet Union and became a focus of cold-war fears about technological supremacy. *Sputnik* set off a race into space between the world's two superpowers—the former Soviet Union and the United States. As a result of the space race, American President Dwight David Eisenhower created a new agency within the Department of Defense, named the Advanced Research Projects Agency, or ARPA. Shortly after its creation, administrators at ARPA began planning to exploit the potential held by developing computer technology. The result was the Advanced Research Projects Agency Network (ARPANET). The first node to be integrated into ARPANET was established at UCLA in 1969. Stanford Research Institute, the University of California at Santa Barbara, and the University of Utah all entered ARPANET later that year. By 1971, there were 15 nodes established, including university, Department of Defense, and commercial computers serving the defense industry. The project became international in 1973 with the establishment of nodes at the University College of London and the Royal Radar Establishment in Norway. The Internet was demonstrated publicly for the first time in October 1972 at the International Computer Communication Conference.

About the same time, the International Network Working Group (INWG)— which grew out of a conference at Sussex University in England in 1973—established standards for developing the Transmission Control Protocol (TCP) and Internet Protocol (IP), commonly known as **TCP/IP**. TCP/IP standards were intended to permit ARPANET computers to communicate efficiently with one another.

TCP/IP: Transmission Control Protocol/Internet Protocol. This protocol, an agreed-upon set of rules directing computers on how to exchange information with each other, is the foundation of the Internet. Other Internet protocols, such as FTP, Gopher, and HTTP, depend on TCP/IP to function.[5]

In 1981, another network that was to play an important role in the development of the Internet was founded. Known as BITNET (Because It's Time Network), this new system was designed specifically to facilitate the use of e-mail and mailing lists. Also in 1981, a network designed to allow computer science departments to communicate with one another was formed. Known as CSNET, it was a creation of the National Science Foundation and also facilitated the exchange of e-mail. In 1987, BITNET and CSNET combined to form CREN, the Corporation for Research and Education Networking.

THE WEB IS BORN

Emerging standards led to quick growth in both CREN and the ARPANET. By the mid-1980s the Internet was born. True to its ARPANET roots, in its early days the Internet linked scientists, university professors, researchers, and software and hardware developers. By 1987, the number of host computers connected to the Internet had reached 10,000. Two years later the number had grown beyond the 100,000 mark, and by 1992 more than 1 million host machines were connected to the Internet. In 1990, ARPANET officially ceased operation. Around the same time, the taboo against commercial use of the Internet began to be replaced with an entrepreneurial spirit as commercial businesses began to establish presences on the Internet as a way of reaching customers. The growth of the Internet is shown in Table 1-1.

The data in Table 1-1 are mostly estimates. They are also a bit dated. Nobody can say exactly how many Web sites are in operation today, or how many people are using the Internet. However, it is estimated that more than 100 million host computers are now in operation,[6] with more than 600 million users around the world.[7] Every 30 minutes, a new network becomes part of the Internet, and that entry time is dropping. Statistics show that the number of Internet users is growing by 15 percent per month. However you look at it, the rate of growth in Internet use continues to be phenomenal!

Host computer: A computer that is accessible via the Internet.

The year 1990 is very important for another reason. It is the year the Web was born! Many people trace the birth of the Web to activities that were under way at the European Laboratory for Particle Physics (CERN) in the 1980s. Located near Geneva, Switzerland, CERN is credited with being the official birthplace of the World Wide Web. In 1984, CERN effectively applied the TCP/IP standards that had been developed nearly a decade earlier by the International Network Working Group. Using object-oriented technology developed by NeXT Software, CERN scientists created the world's first Web server and client machines and introduced their own browser software. CERN's WWW project was tasked with developing a distributed hypermedia system that would allow access in an easy-to-use graphical format from any desktop computer to information from across the world.

Tim Berners-Lee, who worked at CERN, brought together the ideas that made the World Wide Web a reality. Berners-Lee wrote the software that made

TABLE 1-1   The Growth of the Internet

Date	Hosts	Date	Hosts
1969	4	04/92	890,000
04/71	23	07/92	992,000
06/74	62	10/92	1,136,000
03/77	111	01/93	1,313,000
08/81	213	04/93	1,486,000
05/82	235	07/93	1,776,000
08/83	562	10/93	2,056,000
10/84	1,024	01/94	2,217,000
10/85	1,961	07/94	3,212,000
02/86	2,308	10/94	3,864,000
11/86	5,089	01/95	5,846,000
12/87	28,174	07/95	8,200,000
07/88	33,000	01/96	14,352,000
10/88	56,000	07/96	16,729,000
01/89	80,000	01/97	21,819,000
07/89	130,000	07/97	26,053,000
10/89	159,000	01/98	29,670,000
10/90	313,000	07/98	36,739,000
01/91	376,000	01/99	43,230,000
07/91	535,000	07/99	56,218,000
10/91	617,000	01/00	72,398,092
01/92	727,000	07/00	93,047,785

Note: "Hosts" refers to computer systems with registered IP addresses.
Source: Zakon, Robert Hobbes. "Hobbes' Internet Timeline v5.2." Updated November 19, 2000. Accessed February 18, 2001. Web posted at http://info.isoc.org/guest/zakon/Internet/History/HIT.html. Reprinted with permission.

possible the first WWW browser, running under NeXTStep software. He also developed the first WWW server, along with most of the communications software it required. You can read Berners-Lee's original proposal to CERN for development of the WWW at http://www.w3.org/pub/WWW/Proposal. Authored in November of 1990, it is entitled "WorldWideWeb: Proposal for a HyperText Project."

A Web prototype developed by Berners-Lee was first demonstrated in December 1990. The official birth date of the Web, however, is May 17, 1991, for it was on that day that Web-based access to CERN computers was made freely available to all Internet users. The creation of browser software for common operating systems, such as Microsoft Windows and the Apple Operating System, ensured the rapid expansion of the Web.

When President Clinton took office in 1992, his administration placed a high priority on developing what was being called the "information superhighway." The information superhighway was envisioned as a vast network of interconnected computers that would make it possible for everyone to carry out research, send e-mail, shop, and perform a wide variety of daily functions online. Vice President Al Gore focused many of his efforts on developing the information superhighway, and he was successful in gaining passage of the U. S. National Information Infrastructure Act (NIIA) of 1993. The NIIA grew out of the Clinton administration's call to establish a national technology policy for America designed to "invest in a 21st century infrastructure, establish education and training programs for a high skills workforce, empower America's small businesses with technology, enhance industrial performance through critical technology research and development, and create a world class business environment for private sector investment and innovation."[8] Also in 1993, the National Science Foundation created the InterNIC. The InterNIC is a cooperative activity between the National Science Foundation, AT&T, and Network Solutions, Inc. The InterNIC facilitates domain name registration through the **Domain Name System (DNS)**.

Domain names are used to identify a location on the Internet. The domain name for the Web site that supports this guide, for example, is talkjustice.com. You can reach *Talk Justice* on the Web by entering its address into your Web browser. For *Talk Justice*, the address is simply http://talkjustice.com, although you can also use http://www.talkjustice.com if you wish. You can reach the InterNIC itself at the following address: http://www.internic.net. The InterNIC provides services that go beyond domain name registration. (We will have much more to say about using Internet addresses in the next chapter.)

One of the most useful InterNIC services for beginners is *Roadmap*. Developed by Patrick Crispen, *Roadmap* is an online workshop available via a series of 27 e-mail messages. The messages, sent about four times per week, explain in some detail how to navigate the Internet. They are automatically sent to workshop registrants free of charge. The workshop takes about six weeks to complete. Registration instructions for the *Roadmap* workshop are included at the end of this chapter. You might also want to visit Crispin's latest undertaking, the Internet Tourbus, at http://www.tourbus.com. Tourbus calls itself, "the click and clack" of the online world.

Uniform Resource Locator (URL): the address for any location on the Internet or the World Wide Web, expressed in this fashion: http://talkjustice.com or http://www.talkjustice.com.

A domain name functions as a **Uniform Resource Locator**, or URL (although there are also other types of URLs). A URL specifies a location on the

Internet such as the address of a **Web page.** Underlying any URL is a numerical address based on the Internet Protocol. Such numerical addresses are called IP addresses for short. The IP address for a criminology site called crimtoday.com, for example, is 4.36.76.231, and you can reach the crimtoday.com site by using that number in place of its URL (but don't type "www" in front of it, and be sure you get the dots in the right places). A few sites, including some that are used primarily for the dissemination of information within corporations or other organizations, have not registered domain names with the InterNIC and are reachable (if at all) only via their IP addresses.[9] In case you're wondering, multiple domain names can reside on a single IP address, although that rarely happens.

> **Web Page:** a World Wide Web document, usually in HTML format, capable of being displayed by a Web browser.

InterNIC-assigned domain names follow a logical structure. The first part of a domain name, such as "talkjustice," can be almost anything that the site administrator chooses (if the name has not already been registered by someone else). Name extensions, however, indicate the category into which the site falls. When domain name extensions were first developed, sites were categorized into five basic groups, as follows:

.gov	government
.edu	education
.com	commercial
.mil	military
.org	organization

The explosive growth in the number of domain names filed with the InterNIC has led to expansion of the naming system. New extensions, including .aero; .biz; .coop; .info; .museum; .name; .pro, have been approved by the Internet Corporation for Assigned Names and Numbers (ICANN) to more accurately categorize individuals and organizations. A movement toward the use of a two-country extension is also growing (and is already in use in a number of countries). A country extension looks something like this: http://talkjustice.com.us. It indicates that the site called "talkjustice.com" runs from a computer located in the United States. Unfortunately, however, not all country codes have been fully implemented.

WHAT IS THE WORLD WIDE WEB?

As you may have gathered by now, the Internet forms the backbone of the **World Wide Web** (WWW), but the Web is not the Internet. Nor, for that matter, is the Internet the Web. The **Internet,** simply put, consists of a huge number of linked computers that are capable of communicating with one another through certain agreed-upon standards for the transmission of information. These standards, called *protocols*, consist primarily of the Transmission Control Protocol and the Internet Protocol (TCP/IP). TCP/IP allow computers to talk with each other regardless of the software operating system they are running (e.g., Windows, Linux, UNIX, Mac OS, OS2, VMS) or the hardware they use. Hence, by using a shared suite of protocols, desktop computers powered by processors manufactured by companies such as Intel Corporation and running, for example, Windows, can efficiently communicate with VAX machines (e.g., older mainframe computers) running VMS software or with machines powered by Alpha processors running UNIX or Linux software.

World Wide Web (WEB, WWW, W3): a worldwide collection of text and multimedia files and other network services interconnected via a system of hypertext documents residing on computers around the world.

The Internet can also be viewed in terms of the content it is capable of providing to users. Seen this way, the Internet is an information-rich environment supported by a wide variety of functional applications such as e-mail, news, Telnet, FTP, and Gopher (some of which are discussed later in this guide). The World Wide Web is merely another application supported by the Internet, although it has quickly become the most popular application on the Internet. From a technical standpoint, the Web is simply another set of protocols that support rich graphical capabilities. The real significance of the Web lies in the fact that it provided the first graphical user interface (GUI) to the Internet. Whereas the Internet was once a text-only medium, Web protocols have enabled it to support rich graphics, animation, audio, and video.

The communications protocol underlying the Web is termed **HyperText Transfer Protocol (HTTP)**. On the Web, hypertext is a navigational tool linking data objects (like text, graphics, video, and sound) together by association. The links (from one page to another or within pages) form what is essentially a web of pages—hence the use of the term "World Wide Web." Berners-Lee and Cailliau described the process in their original CERN proposal as follows: "A hypertext page has pieces of text which refer to other texts. Such references are highlighted and can be selected with a mouse. . . . When you select a reference, the browser [the software used to access the WWW] presents you with the text which is referenced: you have made the browser follow a hypertext link."[10]

HTTP (HyperText Transfer Protocol): the communications protocol underlying the Web.

HTML (HyperText Markup Language): a programming language used to create Web sites.

The HTTP protocol is supported by a programming language called **HyperText Markup Language (HTML)**. HTML programmers create Web sites consisting of a series of Web pages linked to one another on the same site through hypertext. Hence, clicking on a linked word, phrase, or image will transport you to another Web page. Linked objects appear as highlighted or underlined text or as images on a Web page.

In the old days (just a few years ago, actually), HTML programmers had to work with raw code and had to add every instruction to their Web pages by typing it in on the keyboard. Today, however, page-creation software (e.g., Microsoft's FrontPage®, Adobe's PageMaker®, Claris Corporation's Home Page®, and Symantec Corporation's Visual Page®) automates the process of Web site creation.

The development of the Web also depended on the emergence of **browsers**— software capable of interpreting HTML and presenting it to Web surfers in the form of visually rich, or graphical, information. Because browsers are built around hypertext links, using a browser is a lot like flipping through pages in a book— except that browsers make it possible to go directly to the page you want without having to skim through page after page of hard-copy text!

> **Browser:** a program run on a computer for viewing World Wide Web pages. Examples include Netscape Communicator®, Microsoft Internet Explorer®, MSN Explorer®, and Mosaic.

One of the first Web browsers to receive widespread acceptance was **Mosaic**. Mosaic was developed by the National Center for Supercomputing Applications (NCSA). It was easy to use, was available on UNIX, PC, and Macintosh platforms, and was freely distributed. In April 1994 Netscape Communications Corporation was formed. The company built its popular browser, Netscape Navigator (now called Communicator), using Mosaic software as a base. Other browsers, including the popular Microsoft Internet Explorer (MIE), soon followed.

With the creation of HTML and the invention of Web browsers, the Internet left the era of "naked text" and became capable of communicating to its users rich images, graphics, sound, and even video. Today's Java-based applets, VRML (which supports three-dimensional graphics), and ActiveX technology, are making Web-based motion, sound, and even video commonplace. Other innovative technologies, such as RealAudio® and RealVideo® (now combined in one software product called RealPlayer®) and Macromedia Corporation's Shockwave® plug-ins, are extending the capabilities of browsers into previously unimagined areas. A new form of HTML, known as Dynamic HTML, has enhanced possibilities for Web content. Dynamic HTML can be used to create content that can be changed on the fly, adding greater interactivity to the Web and adding more multimedia capabilities to Web pages. Dynamic HTML is leading to the merging of computers and television, while simultaneously creating a truly interactive environment for the user. Dynamic HTML is supported only by versions 4.0 (and later) of Communicator and Explorer.

Even more recently XML, or eXtensible Markup Language, has been developed by people seeking to improve on HTML. While HTML tells your computer how to *display* a document, XML tells your computer just what that document *is*. So, for example, if you are viewing a document consisting of arrest data that's written exclusively in

HTML, your computer wouldn't know the difference between that document and, say, a recipe for *skordalia* (Greek garlic spread). If the arrest statistics contained hidden XML codes, however, your computer would be able to interpret the document as criminal justice data. The benefit of *that* is that it will (in the near future) allow your computer to automatically manipulate the arrest data (and any other data coded with XML) for the best possible display among varying platforms (from laptops, to Personal Information Managers, to cell phones) and to transparently integrate it into other databases that may already exist on your computer.

WHO RUNS THE WEB?

Any huge, rapidly growing global entity requires careful coordination. Web administration today rests primarily in the hands of the World Wide Web Consortium (W3C), also known as the World Wide Web Initiative. The W3C was founded in 1994 to develop common protocols for the evolution of the World Wide Web. It is an international industry consortium, jointly hosted by the Massachusetts Institute of Technology Laboratory for Computer Science (MIT/LCS) in the United States, the Institut National de Recherche en Informatique et en Automatique (INRIA) in Europe, and the Keio University Shonan Fujisawa Campus in Asia. Initially, the W3C was established in collaboration with CERN.

The consortium is led by Tim Berners-Lee, director of the W3C, and Jean-François Abramatic, chairman of the W3C. It is funded by member organizations and continues to work with the global community to produce specifications and reference software that are made freely available throughout the world. You can reach the World Wide Web Consortium at http://www.w3.org/Consortium.

Another very important group is the Internet Corporation for Assigned Names and Numbers (ICANN), a private non-profit corporation responsible for maintaining and improving the Web domain name system (DNS) and IP address space allocation. You can visit ICANN at http://www.icann.org.

RECOMMENDED READINGS

Web-Based Histories of the Internet

>> Michael Hauben and Ronda Hauben, *Netizens: On the History and Impact of Usenet and the Internet* (a work in progress): http://www.columbia.edu/~hauben/netbook. The most comprehensive work on Internet history on the Web.

>> Barry Leiner, Vinton Cerf, Jon Postel, and others, *A Brief History of the Internet:* http://www.isoc.org/internet-history.

>> *Cosmoslink's Internet History:* http://www.cosmoslink.net/cosmos/tutorial_1.html.

>> Henry Edward Hardy, *Master's Thesis on Internet History* (1993):
   http://info.isoc.org/guest/zakon/Internet/History/History_of_the_Net.html
   and http://www.ocean.ic.net/ftp/doc/nethist.html.

>> Robert Hobbes Zakon, *Hobbes' Internet Timeline*:
   http://info.isoc.org/guest/zakon/Internet/History/HIT.html.

>> *Internet History and WWW History*:
   http://www.vissing.dk/Internet.History/ihistlist.html.

>> Public Broadcasting System, *Internet Timeline*: http://www.pbs.org/
   internet/timeline.

Web-Based Guides to the Internet

>> Patrick Crispen, *Internet Roadmap*—a free, 27-lesson, self-paced workshop
   on the World Wide Web. Crispen's workshop is written mostly for beginners and is delivered in an easy-to-follow, entertaining series of e-mail messages. See the HTML version of *Roadmap* at:
   http://edie.cprost.sfu.ca/Roadmap/Welcome.html.

>> Patrick Crispen and Bob Rankin, *Internet Tourbus*—this site explains
   Internet technology in plain English with a dash of humor thrown in:
   http://www.tourbus.com.

>> Microsoft Corporation, *The Complete Internet Guide and Web Tutorial*—an
   excellent overview of almost all aspects of today's Internet, including Web
   surfing, e-mail, and site building: http://www.microsoft.com/insider/inter-
   net/default.htm.

>> *Newbie Net*—"where Newbies become Knowbies...":
   http://www.newbie.net.

Books

>> Robert Cailliau and James Gillies, *How the Web Was Born: The Story of the
   World Wide Web* (New York: Oxford University Press, 2000).

>> Katie Hafner and Matthew Lyon, *Where Wizards Stay Up Late: The Origins
   of the Internet* (New York: Touchstone Books, 1998).

>> John Naughton, *A Brief History of the Future: Origins of the Internet* (New
   York: Overlook Press, 2000).

>> Peter Salus, *Casting the Net: From ARPANET to Internet and Beyond* (New
   York: Addison Wesley, 1995).

>> Stephen Segaller, *Nerds 2.0.1: A Brief History of the Internet* (New York: TV
   Books, 1999).

>> Art Wolinsky, *The History of the Internet and the World Wide Web* (2000).
   Note: this is an elementary introduction, suitable for teaching children
   about the Web.

Surfing the Web

The Web reminds me of early days of the PC
industry. No one really knows anything. All
experts have been wrong.

—*Steve Jobs,* Wired[11]

He who travels much knows much.

—*Thomas Fuller,* Gnomologia

CHAPTER OUTLINE

MAKING THE CONNECTION

Before you can begin to browse the Web you will need certain kinds of hardware and software. Almost any computer (and even many cellular phones and Personal Information Managers) is capable of receiving information from the Internet, although not all can run the latest software that makes surfing the Web a pleasant experience. For a fast connection and for a machine that supports the most capable browsers, you will probably want to use a newer computer. If you are using a PC, you can install capable Web browsers on an older 486-type machine running Windows 3.1. For better performance, however, you will want a Pentium-based machine. Pentium III's, Pentium IV's, and later-generation processors will give you better satisfaction than earlier models.

Before you can connect to the Web you will need an Internet connection. Internet connections take a variety of forms, from those provided by **online services** to **dial-up connections** to **direct connections**. Online services, such as America Online, require registered users to pay a monthly fee. They have established telephone numbers in most areas that allow users to connect to the service. Once logged on to the online service, users are able to browse a wide variety of information sources, message forums, and software libraries provided by the service. America Online and other online services have incorporated e-mail programs, newsreaders, and Web browsers into their proprietary software so that registered users can send and receive e-mail, transfer files between computers on the Internet, browse the Web, participate in newsgroup discussions, and even create their own Web pages. On-line services provide Internet access without requiring users to have a direct connection to the Internet or to sign up for service through an Internet service provider.

An online service, however, may not be your first choice. If you are working through a university's computer system (most likely a local area network, or LAN), the system may have a high-speed (or direct) connection to the Internet. If so, accessing the Web will be a simple matter of starting the browser installed on the machine you are using (assuming one is available) and typing in the URL of the site you want to visit.

If you do not have a direct connection and you have not joined an online service, you will probably need to establish a dial-up connection to the Internet. A dial-up connection requires a modem and an **Internet service provider (ISP)**. ISPs are companies that complete the dial-up connection between your computer's modem and the Internet, allowing you to browse the Web, read newsgroups, and send and receive e-mail. Depending on where you live, a large number of ISPs may be available in your area. If you live in a relatively remote area, however, your choice of ISPs may be limited—or you may need to make a long-distance telephone call in order to connect with an ISP of your choice.

Pricing, features, and dependability of ISPs vary widely. One easy way to select an ISP is to use a service provided by Netscape Communications Corporation called ISP Select. ISP Select can help you find the ISP that's best for you. The service allows you to compare the prices and services of a variety of ISPs, create new ISP accounts, and get and configure the software you need to connect to the ISP of your choice. ISP Select is available via Netscape Communications Corporation at the following address:

http://home.netscape.com/assist/isp_select

You may also choose to connect to the Internet through a cable modem (if such service is available in your area), a satellite connection (which requires you to install a small dish for sending and receiving signals from a satellite), or ISDN or DSL lines. Because these are rather specialized connections and are often quite expensive, we will not discuss them here. However, even people who connect to the Internet through cutting-edge technology still need to sign up with an ISP as an intermediary.

Once you are connected to the Internet, your machine becomes a **client computer**. The machine to which you are connected is called a host machine, a server, or a **Web server**. At this point you are ready to begin surfing (usually pronounced "surfin'"), or browsing, the Web!

CHOOSING YOUR BROWSER

Today's browser software comes down to what is essentially a choice between two major competitors: Netscape Communicator (also known as Netscape Navigator) and Microsoft Internet Explorer (MSIE). Although it is possible to get satisfactory results with earlier versions of both browsers (or other browsers, for that matter), this guide will assume that you are running Netscape Communicator version 6 or later (which we will refer to simply as "Communicator") or Microsoft Internet Explorer 5.5 or later (which we will refer to as "Explorer"). Both programs are freely available for download via the Internet and are relatively easy to install on your computer. If you already have an Internet connection, but are not running the latest browser, we recommend that you download and install a copy now.

To download Internet Explorer, go to:

http://www.microsoft.com/ie

To download Netscape Communicator, go to:

http://www.netscape.com

If you are working on a PC, both Communicator and Explorer run best under Windows 95, Windows 98, Windows 2000, Windows Me, Windows NT, or

Windows XP. Explorer can be tightly integrated with the Windows operating system and can make your desktop into a kind of "Web space," or a virtual extension of the World Wide Web. It can also be run as a stand-alone program.

ONCE YOU'RE CONNECTED: USING YOUR BROWSER

Once you're connected to the Internet, the first thing you are likely to do is use your browser to navigate the Web. Four major navigational features are available on most browsers:

>> URLs
>> Navigational buttons
>> Internal and external hyperlinks (e.g., images, text, video, and sound)
>> Bookmarks

Figure 2-1 shows these features as they appear in Netscape Communicator (version 6). Figure 2-2 illustrates the same features in Microsoft's Internet Explorer (version 5.5). Each navigational feature will be discussed in the pages that follow.

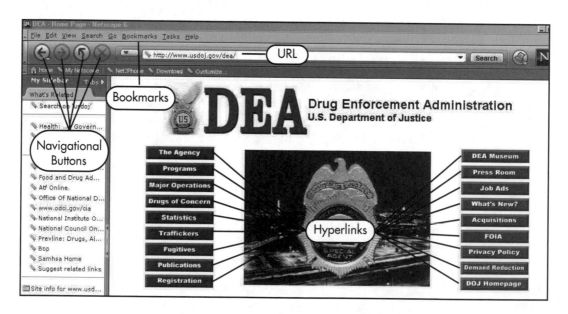

FIGURE 2-1

Navigational features available in Netscape Communicator (release 6).
Netscape Communicator browser window © 1999 Netscape Communications Corporation. Used with permission. Netscape Communications has not authorized, sponsored, endorsed, or approved this publication and is not responsible for its content.

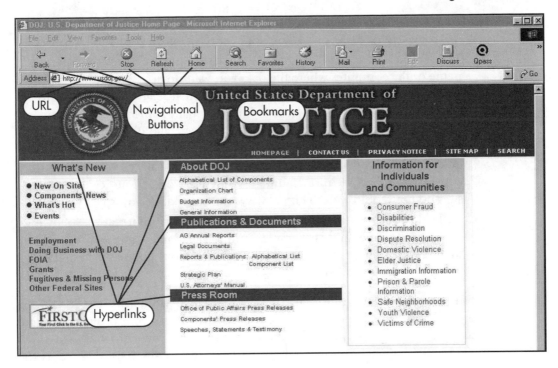

FIGURE 2-2
Navigational features available in Microsoft Internet Explorer (version 5.5).
Navigational features available in Microsoft Internet Explorer. Reprinted with permission of Microsoft Corporation.

URLs

As mentioned earlier, URL is an acronym for Uniform Resource Locator. URLs specify addresses/locations on the Internet and help you get where you want to go. Most URLs take the form http://www.prenhall.com/schmalleger. In this example, the URL has three parts, separated by slashes.

1. The first part of a URL (before the two slashes) tells your browser the type of resource at the address you are about to specify and the method to use to access that resource. In this case, "http" (which stands for HyperText Transfer Protocol) tells your browser that it is being instructed to load and display a hypertext document. When you type in a URL, most contemporary browsers assume that you intend to enter the "http" prefix, thus making it unnecessary to do so. In place of "http" you could enter "ftp," "mailto," "gopher," "telnet," "news," and other commands. You could even enter a

"file" command, telling your browser to open a file located on a local hard drive (that is, one that resides on your machine or on your local network).

2. The second part of any URL that begins with "http" specifies the Internet name of the computer where the data you want to access is located. In this case, the second part is www.prenhall.com, which refers your browser to the World Wide Web, where it is to find a domain named "prenhall.com." "Prenhall.com" is the domain name of Prentice Hall Publishing Company's World Wide Web server. (Prentice Hall is the company that publishes this guide, and its products are often available electronically as well as in hard copy.) As you become more familiar with URLs you will notice that *some* sites do not require you to enter "www" in the address you specify.

3. URLs that begin with "http" usually have additional information following the domain name. In this example, "schmalleger" refers to the directory on the Prentice Hall server in which information about popular criminal justice textbooks is located.

It is worthwhile noting that we have chosen to work with a URL that is generic. That is, we have not specified any particular file for your browser to open. Once it reaches the indicated location on the Web, your browser will open whichever file the site creators (or Webmasters) at that site have defined as the starting page.

It is possible for us to be more specific, telling our browser to open a particular file. You could, for example, enter the following URL in your browser:

http://www.prenhall.com/schmalleger/crim2day/index.html

This URL will cause your browser to load a file named "index.html" ("html" or "htm" is an extension indicating a file written in HyperText Markup Language) in a subdirectory named "crim2day" (which, knowing that this is a publisher's site, probably means that it holds files for a specific project or textbook), which in turn is part of a directory named "schmalleger" within the Prentice Hall domain on the World Wide Web. In this example, "crim2day" is, in fact, the directory of *Criminology Today*, a popular introductory criminology textbook. Keep in mind, however, that we often may not know what files exist at a given site and that file names may change far more quickly than site names. Hence, the best choice may be to begin with the default file that loads at a location we are interested in.

To summarize what we have said, we can think of a URL as specifying a *protocol*, followed by (1) a *domain* address to which you wish to connect, (2) the *directory* within that domain that you wish to access, and (3) the *file* that you wish to view or locate. Hence, a generic way of thinking about URLs would be as follows:

protocol://domain name/directory name/file name

Some useful tips to remember about URLs include the following:

>> A URL contains no spaces.

>> A URL always uses right-leaning (forward) slashes—that is, slashes that slant to the right.

>> The first slash in any URL is always a double slash, preceded by a colon.

>> Do not capitalize the protocol. For example, "http" should always be lowercase. Keep in mind, however, that some URLs contain capital letters. Depending on the kind of server you are trying to contact, it may be necessary to type those letters as capitals (in other cases, either lowercase or capital letters will do, since they will all be interpreted as lowercase).

>> If you can't reach the site you are trying to connect with, check the URL carefully to be sure that you have typed it correctly. One wrong character, one out-of-place period or slash, can break an otherwise successful connection.

>> Although you will often see URLs with *ending* forward slashes, you do not need to type them.

>> Once you have reached a site and have loaded a page, you can find the URL to any link on that page simply by passing your mouse pointer over the link. You will see the pointer turn into a hand, and the URL will appear in the browser's status bar (usually located at the bottom left of your screen).

One way to enter a URL in your browser is to type it into the **location window** just under the **toolbar.** Placement of the location window is shown in Figures 2-1 and 2-2. Most popular browsers keep track of sites you've visited and allow you to return easily. To do so in Explorer, just click on the history icon in the toolbar. You will see a list of places you've recently visited. Click on the one to which you wish to return, and Explorer will take you there without your having to retype the URL for that location. You can do the same thing in Communicator by clicking on the "Go" command above the toolbar icons. For most browsers, however, the history feature applies only to your current session. Once you close your browser, such history information about the sites you've visited is lost.

Today's browsers are smart, in the sense that they remember the URLs of sites you've visited—even from previous sessions. If you begin to type a URL into the location window for a site that you visited a couple of days ago, for example, your browser will fill out the rest of the URL for you. If the browser's "guess" as to where you want to go is wrong, simply continue typing until you have entered the correct URL.

Browsers are smart in another way. Generally, when you view a page containing a link that you've already visited, the hypertext words will appear in a different color—usually red or pink. You can revisit the site by clicking on the link whose color has changed.

Navigational Buttons

Common navigational buttons in most browsers include "forward," "back," "reload" (or "refresh"), "home," and "stop." Navigational buttons are used primarily to help you retrace your steps. If, for example, you viewed a page that you liked, but then went on to visit other sites, you could use the "back" button to return to previously visited pages. After locating those pages, you could then use the "forward" button to get back to where you were. The "forward" and "back" buttons can move you speedily through sites you have already visited because much of the information your browser needs to display a page is stored in the browser's **cache**. It stays there long after you have viewed that page. Cache contents are periodically deleted, so you can't count on navigational buttons to take you back to sites visited long ago. Nonetheless, the "forward" and "back" buttons provide a convenient way of quickly navigating sites you've already visited during the current session.

Other navigational buttons include "stop" and "reload." Clicking the "stop" button tells your browser to abort the loading process. You may want to use the stop button if you change your mind about visiting a site or if a site seems to be taking too long to load. Delays in loading a Web page can have a number of causes, including a slow modem, a bad telephone connection, a busy Web, a slow site, or a stalled connection. If you are experiencing a stalled connection, you may have no way of knowing it—except that the page you are trying to load never arrives at your computer. In that case, clicking "stop" and then "reload" (or "refresh" in Explorer) may be your best choice. A word of caution: The Web can be notoriously slow when filled with users (they don't call it the "World Wide Wait" for nothing). Don't get into the habit of clicking the "stop" and "reload" buttons frequently because doing so starts the process of loading a page all over again. That can take far more time than waiting for a page from a busy site.

You can also use the reload button to update a page. If you viewed a page a few minutes ago and then return to it using your "back" button, the contents of the page may have changed. This is especially true for pages like those found in the *Talk Justice* message forums (discussed later in this guide), where people are constantly posting new messages. Since your browser loads a previously viewed page from your cache, it may be necessary to hit the "reload" button when visiting some pages in order to see updated content. With pages that change only infrequently, this process is rarely necessary.

Internal and External Hyperlinks

You can think of Web pages as electronic files stored on computers located all over the world. Web pages, as mentioned earlier, are really HTML documents. As such they generally contain a number of hyperlinks. Hyperlinks provide a way of jumping between pages and between sites. Clicking on a hyperlink will take you to the spot designated by the Web designer who created the page you are using.

> **Hyperlink:** a connection between two anchors, or locations, on the Web. Clicking on one anchor will take you to the linked anchor. Hyperlinks can refer to anchors within the same document, page, or site, or to totally different documents in widely varying locations.

You can tell which text on a page is linked to another page (or which text is "hot") by looking at its color. Links generally appear in a color different from the rest of the text (usually blue) and they are normally underlined. Keep in mind, however, that graphic images can also be links to other content. When you move your cursor over a text link or over a graphic link, your cursor will change from an arrow to a hand.

Bookmarks

You can keep track of URLs that are of special interest to you by using bookmarks. **Bookmarks** are available in Explorer by clicking on the icon marked "Favorites." In Communicator the bookmark feature is plainly labeled "Bookmarks." You can instruct your browser to add sites to your bookmarks. Doing so will create a personalized menu of listed URLs that you can use as shortcuts. To add a site to bookmarks in Communicator, click on the Bookmarks selection and then click "Add Bookmark." This procedure will add the site you are visiting to the bookmark menu.

> **Bookmark:** a pointer to a particular Web site. Within browsers, you can bookmark interesting pages so that you can return to them easily.

You can also create categories to contain your bookmarks, and you can organize your bookmarks by category. Once you have created categories (or folders) for your bookmarks, you can click on "Bookmarks" and then "File Bookmark" in order to place the URL of the site you are visiting in a selected category. In Explorer, the process for adding bookmarks is similar. Just click on "Favorites" and then "Add." Explorer also gives you the choice "Organize," which you can use to create new categories and to move URLs between categories. In Communicator, you can organize your bookmarks by clicking "Bookmarks," then "Manage Bookmarks." Like Explorer, Communicator allows you to drag and drop URLs in order to move them between categories.

As you learn more about bookmarks, you will see that they can be used to create a personalized Web page that you can store on your computer and open with your browser. Doing so is easiest with Communicator, which stores bookmarks in a file called "bookmark.html" in your Netscape 6\defaults subdirectory. You can tell any Web browser to open a "bookmark.htm" file created by

Communicator, and in doing so you will find a handy listing of all sites that you have bookmarked. Figure 2-3 shows a screen capture of a bookmark file used at the Justice Research Association (JRA is the sponsor of this manual) for easy access to frequently visited criminal justice sites. Once opened in any browser, clicking on a selection within this file will take the user directly to the site chosen.

Preferences on browsers at JRA are set to load personalized bookmark files at startup directly from the user's machine. You can set preferences in your browser to either open a file on your machine at startup or to open any file you specify—even one on the Web. You might, for example, set your browser to open the file containing the *Talk Justice* Cybrary Top 100 links (which are partially listed in the next chapter) when it starts. To do so in Communicator, you would click on "Edit" in the toolbar, then select "Preferences," click on "Navigator," **"home page,"** and then enter the URL of the home page you wish to use in the field labeled "Location." If you want to use the *Talk Justice* Cybrary as your browser's default opening page, you would enter http://talkjustice.com/cybrary.asp. (You must, of course, be logged on to the Internet in order to reach this page.) Doing the same thing in Explorer requires you to click on "Tools," "Internet Options," "General," and then to fill in the selection labeled "home page" with the URL or name of the file you wish to load at startup. Keep in mind that if the file is on your computer you must specify a complete path to the file, not just the name of the file. You can easily do so by using the "browse" button next to the "home page" selection on most browsers.

Home page: the first or opening page of a Web site. Also, the Web site that automatically loads each time you launch your browser.

Here's a more detailed description of how to set home pages in Communicator and Explorer, using the *Talk Justice* Cybrary as an example:

Communicator 6

1. At the top of your browser, click on "Edit."
2. Then click on "Preferences."
3. See where it says "Home page"? Fill in the "location" box with http://talkjustice.com/cybrary.asp
4. Click OK.
5. You're done!

Internet Explorer 5.5

1. At the top of your browser, click on "Tools."
2. Then click on "Internet Options."

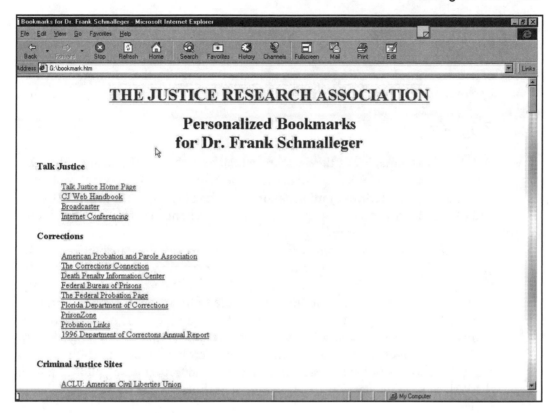

FIGURE 2-3
The start of a personalized bookmark file in HTML format. This one belongs to Dr. Frank Schmalleger, Director of the Justice Research Association.

3. Then click on the folder heading that says "General."
4. Enter http://talkjustice.com/cybrary.htm in the box that says "Address."
5. Click "OK."
6. You're done!

If you don't set a home page preference, then most browsers, on starting up, will immediately take you to their own predefined home page. Communicator, for example, will first take you to the Netscape home page. Internet Explorer (MSIE) is set to automatically take you to Microsoft's Web site. If you decide to disable these default features and specify your own home page, you can still click on the large "N" on the right side of Communicator's toolbar to reach the Netscape home page at any time. Similarly, from within Explorer you can click on the large blue "E" or spinning globe (depending on which version of the browser you are running) in the upper right corner to reach the Microsoft home page (this feature is disabled in some versions of Explorer).

A final note: If you have specified a home page of your own, you can return to it at any time by clicking on "home" in the toolbar of either Communicator or Explorer.

Plug-Ins

Web browsers, amazing as they are, are actually capable of displaying only a few types of data. Prior to the release of Netscape Navigator 2.0, browsers could recognize only limited forms of information, including (1) plain text (2) HTML data, and (3) certain image types such as Graphics Interchange Format (GIF) and Joint Photographic Experts Group (JPEG) files.

Helper applications (small programs that extend the capabilities of Web browsers[12]) were needed to use other types of information, such as video or audio files. Prior to the availability of modern browsers, it was necessary for anyone surfing the Web to download an audio or video file to his or her computer, and then run a helper application that could read it. Helper applications are software programs that are external to browsers and that are used to play or view files locally. A common helper application today is Adobe Acrobat Reader®, a software program that allows you to view pages of text as graphics—permitting publication on the Web of page images that are essentially snapshots of the original printed document.

A number of previously popular helper applications have recently been replaced with **plug-ins**. Plug-ins are software applications that are seamlessly integrated into your browser and that allow you to open a wide variety of file types, such as video and audio. Because plug-ins act as though they are a part of your browser, they allow Web page designers to embed sounds, video, and multimedia effects into their Web sites, permitting you to view or hear such special effects in what appears to be a seamless fashion.

> **Plug-ins:** add-on programs designed to work seamlessly with your browser and to enhance its capabilities.

Although hundreds of plug-ins exist for most popular browsers, the data formats most of them support are rarely used. A few plug-ins, however, are virtually essential for avid Web surfers. Important and widely used plug-ins include RealPlayer (which incorporates both audio and video players), Shockwave® or Flash® (to view animations), QuickTime® (to watch video), Window's Media Player™ (for MSIE), Cosmo Player® and Netscape's Live3D® (for three-dimensional graphics). A special form of plug-in technology has been created by Microsoft Corporation. Called

ActiveX®, this proprietary technology is designed to work primarily with Microsoft's Internet Explorer browser.

One of the most essential plug-ins for browsing the Web is RealPlayer. The latest version plays the audio and video files found on many Web sites. You can download a free version of RealPlayer directly from the RealPlayer home page at the following address:

http://www.realplayer.com

You can also download RealPlayer software from many sites that use Real Networks technology. Most such sites display a RealPlayer icon on which you can click to go to the download site. The icon looks something like this:

FIGURE 2-4
One of the most essential plug-ins for browsing the Web is RealPlayer, which is a registered trademark of RealNetworks.

Many people consider Macromedia's Shockwave and Flash plug-ins essential additions to a Web browser. Download Shockwave, or the newer Flash Player, from Macromedia at the following address:

http://www.macromedia.com

They can also be downloaded from any site displaying the Shockwave or Flash icons. If you download RealPlayer version 8.0 or higher from the RealPlayer site, you will find that Flash Player comes with it.

Some of today's most popular plug-ins are bundled with browsers and are seamlessly integrated from the user's point of view. Almost all of today's plug-ins are available at one central Web location called Plug-in Plaza. Plug-in Plaza makes plug-ins available by category, including the following:

>> MultiMedia
>> Graphics
>> Sound
>> Document Viewers
>> Productivity Plug-Ins (such as map viewers and spell checkers)
>> VRML/3-D Plug-Ins

Plug-in Plaza can be reached on the Web at:

http://browserwatch.internet.com/plug-in.html

USING THE WEB

Visit the Microsoft and Netscape sites on the Web at the following addresses:

>> Microsoft: http://www.microsoft.com

>> Netscape: http://www.netscape.com

Then do the following:

1. Write a page about each of these sites, describing what features are available at both. Compare the sites. Which site do you like better? Why?

2. Find the page that allows you to download a free copy of the latest version of Communicator. Find the page that allows you to download a free copy of the latest version of Explorer. Read about the features of both programs. Which sounds better to you? Why?

3

Criminology and Criminal Justice Sites on the Web

While a number of my colleagues remain skeptical about the role the Internet will play in the future of criminal justice and criminal justice education, it is obvious that the Net is the most significant communication tool ever devised, one with world changing potential.

—Cecil Greek, Webmaster, Florida State University, School of Criminology[13]

CHAPTER OUTLINE

SURF'S UP

Once you have established an Internet connection and have your Web browser up and running, it is time to begin the journey through **cyberspace**.

> **Cyberspace:** the computer-created matrix of virtual possibilities, including Web sites, online services, e-mail, discussion groups, and newsgroups, wherein human beings interact with each other and with technology itself.

A fantastic place to begin any Web-based excursion in criminology or criminal justice is the home page of the National Criminal Justice Reference Service (NCJRS). NCJRS describes itself as "a federally sponsored information clearinghouse for people around the country and the world involved with research, policy, and practice related to criminal and juvenile justice and drug control." It is one of the most extensive sources of information available anywhere on crime statistics, crime prevention, and research and evaluation in the area of crime control. The site also provides links to many other sites with information on victimology, juvenile justice, and international criminology. NCJRS serves an international community of policymakers and professionals, and you can be among them by pointing your browser at the NCJRS home page, which is located at http://www.ncjrs.org.

Using NCJRS

NCJRS makes an excellent criminal justice Web starting point because it is essentially a collection of clearinghouses supporting all bureaus of the U. S. Department of Justice (DOJ), Office of Justice Programs (OJP), the National Institute of Justice (NIJ), the Office of Juvenile Justice and Delinquency Prevention (OJJDP), the Bureau of Justice Statistics (BJS), the Bureau of Justice Assistance (BJA), the Office for Victims of Crime (OVC), and the OJP Program Offices. It also supports the Office of National Drug Control Policy (ONDCP), home of our nation's cabinet-level "drug czar," and provides a list of extensive links to other criminal justice and criminology-related information on the Web.

When you arrive at the NCJRS home page, you will find that it is arranged by topical areas, each of which is clickable. A portion of the NCJRS home page can be seen in Figure 3-1.

The NCJRS home page contains a number of clickable selections. Major selections are (1) corrections, (2) courts, (3) drugs and crime, (4) international, (5) juvenile justice, (6) law enforcement, (7) victims of crime, (8) statistics, (9) grants and funding, and (10) an events calendar. Current highlights appear in the middle of the page.

Each selection leads to a number of hypertext links. Clicking on "Law Enforcement," for example, brings up a long list of full-text federal publications

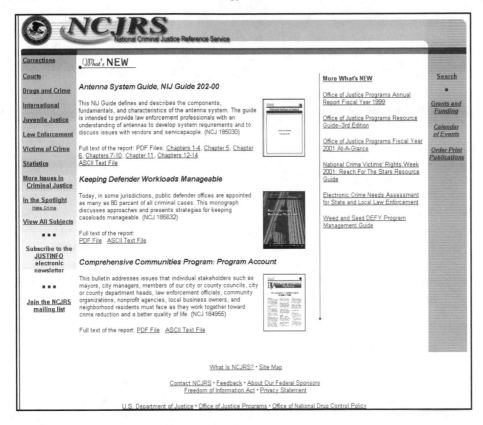

FIGURE 3-1
The home page of the National Criminal Justice Reference Service. You can reach it at http://www.ncjrs.org.

dealing with policing. It also opens up a submenu with many additional choices, such as community policing, computer-related crime, crime mapping, criminal investigation, evidence, law enforcement communications, less-than-lethal technologies, and police discipline and misconduct—just to name a few. Links to other law enforcement-related sites also appear, along with a "Search" choice. If you click "Search" you will be offered what are essentially two choices: (1) a search of the NCJRS Abstracts Database, and (2) an online search of full-text publications. Searching the NCJRS database reveals the site's real depth. The database contains nearly 200,000 documents, published either by the federal government, the states, or by non-profit agencies and for-profit commercial publishers. It contains summaries of criminal justice literature—government reports, journal articles, books, and more. Click on "Search the NCJRS Abstracts Database," enter a keyword or phrase in the search box, and you will typically receive a huge list of annotated publication descriptions in the results that are returned.

If you want to focus your search only on those full-text documents that are available through NCJRS, select "Search online full-text publications." Although this database is much smaller (containing "only" around 2,000 documents from NCJRS partner agency Web sites), it is like having a virtual criminal justice library at your fingertips. Note that many full-text NCJRS documents are available in Adobe Acrobat® format, and you will need to have Adobe Reader installed in order to read them. Pick up a free copy of Acrobat Reader at http://www.adobe.com.

NCJRS regularly publishes an electronic newsletter called *Justice Information* (or JUSTINFO), which details current events, upcoming meetings, ongoing and recently published research, and new developments in the justice field. As discussed in Chapter 5, you can subscribe to JUSTINFO electronically by visiting NCJRS, clicking on "Subscribe to the JUSTINFO electronic newsletter," and entering your name and e-mail address on the form that appears. If you have any problems using NCJRS, you can send e-mail to "Tell NCJRS!" at the following address: tellncjrs@ncjrs.org. You should receive an answer within 48 hours. More information on sending and receiving e-mail can be found in Chapter 4.

The JRA Image Map of the CJ System

Another excellent starting point for Web-based criminal justice explorations is an image map created by the Justice Research Association at its *Talk Justice* site. The map, which is reproduced in black and white in Figure 3-2, can be viewed online at http://talkjustice.com/cjmap.htm. The diagram used in designing the map has been turned into a hot-linked image. Clicking on areas within the image will take you to resources related to those areas. Clicking on "arrest" within the map, for example, leads you to a number of police and civil liberties links. A note of caution is in order when working with image maps: Not all browsers support them, although all recent versions of Communicator and Explorer do.

SITE LISTINGS

The NCJRS and *Talk Justice* sites, comprehensive as they may be, are only two of many interesting criminal justice sites on the Web. The Web is literally awash in sites that should be of interest to anyone in the field of criminology or criminal justice. The remaining pages in this chapter provide a list of such sites. Although space won't permit including all criminology and criminal justice sites, a representative collection of some of the most popular sites is provided here. Sites are drawn from those listed on "Dr. Frank Schmalleger's Cybrary," an information-rich site known as "The World's Criminal Justice Directory." The Cybrary's (the word means "cyber-library") central feature is an annotated and fully searchable

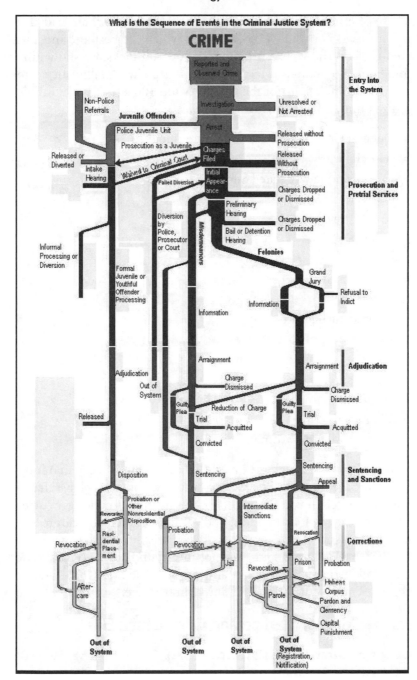

FIGURE 3-2
The Talk Justice Image Map. Adapted from the Bureau of Justice Statistics.
Modified image courtesy of Cecil Greek.

database of crime and justice sites that numbers more than 12,000. The Cybrary also features a "Top 100 Picks" section in which the best and most useful justice-related sites on the Web can be found. Top 100 Picks are shown in this manual with a "Top 100" icon next to them. (Visit http://www.talkjustice.com/top100.asp to view the complete list of the Cybrary's top 100 sites.) Links in this chapter are organized under the following headings:

>> General Criminal Justice and Criminology Sites
>> Associations
>> Courts and Law-Related Sites
>> Corrections Sites
>> Crime Prevention
>> Forensics
>> Gangs
>> International Resources
>> Justice Statistics
>> Juvenile Justice Sites
>> Law Enforcement Resources
>> Live Feeds from Police Scanners
>> Terrorism
>> Unsolved Crimes
>> Victims of Crime
>> Violence Against Women

As you work through the links listed in this guide, keep in mind that the Web is a dynamic medium. URLs change constantly. Some may have changed since this guide was printed. If you find a URL in this list that is no longer current, check the Cybrary for the latest listings and updates. Remember, you can reach the Cybrary at http://talkjustice.com/cybrary.asp. If you wish to tell the Cybrary staff about a URL that has changed but has not been updated recently, send e-mail to admin@talkjustice.com. You can also recommend sites to be added by clicking "Submit a Link" at the bottom of any Cybrary page.

General Criminal Justice and Criminology Sites

Bureau of Justice Assistance (BJA)
http://www.ojp.usdoj.gov/BJA

The Bureau of Justice Assistance (BJA), a component of the Office of Justice Programs, U. S. Department of Justice, supports innovative programs that strengthen the nation's criminal justice system by assisting state and local governments in combating violence.

Court TV   http://www.courttv.com

The Web version of this popular television network provides visitors with complete coverage of significant criminal trials, as well as a crime library, live chat, message boards, and crime news.

Crime.com   http://www.crime.com

Crime.com's goal is the premier media brand for interactive crime information, news, and entertainment, as well as a local community information network that will enable users to contact neighborhood watch participants, local law enforcement agencies and other related groups that share a common concern for overseeing safety in a particular geographic area.

 Crime Spider—a crime and justice search engine
http://crimespider.com

A crime and justice Internet search engine offering information on a wide range of sites, including cybercrime, industrial espionage, detectives, domestic violence, private investigations, criminalistics, and so on.

 CrimeLynx—The Criminal Defense Practitioner's Guide through the Internet   http://www.crimelynx.com

Contains a legal resource center with research links, links to experts, investigation links, and crime policy links. A criminal justice center with media links, shopping, and chat is also available onsite.

 The Cybrary (The World's Criminal Justice Directory)
http://talkjustice.com/cybrary.asp

The world's largest collection of crime and justice links all in one place. The Cybrary database contains more than 12,000 fully searchable links.

 Florida State University's criminal justice resource site
http://www.criminology.fsu.edu/cj.html

One of the oldest criminal justice resources on the Web, this site contains links to many other crime and justice sites.

 MegaLinks in Criminal Justice   http://faculty.ncwc.edu/toconnor

A very comprehensive site where you can find just about anything related to crime and law enforcement.

National Criminal Justice Reference Service (NCJRS)
http://www.ncjrs.org

The National Criminal Justice Reference Service is one of the most extensive sources of information on criminal and juvenile justice in the world, providing services to an international community of policymakers and professionals.

 ### National Institute of Justice (NIJ)
http://www.ojp.usdoj.gov/nij

Sponsoring agency of the National Criminal Justice Reference Service. The National Institute of Justice is a component of the Office of Justice Programs, which also includes the Bureau of Justice Assistance, Bureau of Justice Statistics, Office of Science and Technology and Sentencing and Adjudication Program.

 ### Talk Justice   http://talkjustice.com

Talk Justice is the nation's premier criminal justice discussion forum. Offering a number of message boards, it is available for use by students, professors, professionals, and interested citizens.

 ### U. S. Department of Justice Home Page (DOJ)
http://www.usdoj.gov

The mission of the U. S. Department of Justice is to enforce the law, to provide federal leadership in preventing and controlling crime, and to seek just punishment for those guilty of unlawful behavior.

The Virtual Encyclopedia of Crime and Law Enforcement
http://www.refdesk.com/crime.html

This site offers a comprehensive collection of crime news and in-depth information surrounding famous cases around the country. Read autopsy reports, search warrants, FBI files, and more.

Associations

 ### Academy of Criminal Justice Sciences (ACJS)
http://www.acjs.org

The Academy of Criminal Justice Sciences is an international organization established in 1963 to foster professional and scholarly activities in the field of criminal justice. ACJS currently has over 3,800 active members.

American Academy of Forensic Sciences   http://www.aafs.org

The American Academy of Forensic Sciences is a professional society dedicated to the application of science to the law.

American Bar Association (ABA)   http://www.abanet.org

Home page of the largest and most influential national association of attorneys. Information about the positions taken by the association and model ethics rules are available at this site.

American Board of Criminalists
http://www.criminalistics.com/ABC

The American Board of Criminalists provides a peer-developed and peer-reviewed certification program, based on assessment of competency using written examinations and proficiency testing.

American Civil Liberties Union (ACLU)   http://www.aclu.org

The American Civil Liberties Union is the nation's foremost advocate of individual rights—litigating, legislating, and educating the public on a broad array of issues affecting individual freedom in the United States.

American Correctional Association (ACA)
http://www.corrections.com/aca

Web site of the American Correctional Association, a multi-disciplinary organization of professionals representing all facets of corrections and criminal justice—including federal, state, and military correctional facilities and prisons, county jails, and detention centers.

American Jail Association   http://www.corrections.com/aja

Home page of the American Jail Association. The site provides a wealth of information about jails.

American Judicature Society   http://www.ajs.org

Primary areas of focus are judicial independence, ethics in the courts, judicial selection, the jury, court administration, and public understanding of the justice system.

American Probation & Parole Association (APPA)
http://www.appa-net.org

APPA is an international association composed of individuals from the United States and Canada actively involved with probation, parole, and community-based corrections, in both adult and juvenile sectors.

American Society for Industrial Security (ASIS)
http://www.asisonline.org

Online security resources from the American Society for Industrial Security (ASIS).

American Society of Criminology (ASC)
http://www.asc41.com

World Wide Web site of the American Society of Criminology. The ASC is the pre-eminent organization of academic, theoretical, and applied criminology in the United States.

 International Association of Chiefs of Police (IACP)
http://www.theiacp.org

The International Association of Chiefs of Police is the world's oldest and largest non-profit membership organization of police executives, with over 16,000 members in over 95 different countries.

Courts and Law-Related Sites

 Cornell University's Legal Information Institute (LII)
http://www.law.cornell.edu

A starting point for Cornell University's Legal Information Institute. The site offers numerous legal resources, and is one of the best free sites on the Web for anyone researching the law and court opinions.

 Court TV   http://www.courttv.com

Web site of the Court TV network. The site contains information about the network, including the full text of oral arguments for the many trials they cover.

 Courts.Net   http://www.courts.net

This site provides directory listings for courts across the United States.

Federal Judicial Center (FJC)   http://www.fjc.gov

The Federal Judicial Center is the research and education agency of the federal judicial system.

Federal Judiciary   http://www.uscourts.gov

Home page of the Administrative Office of the U. S. courts.

 Find Law   http://www.findlaw.com

Extensive collection of legal information. Ranges from links to state and federal court cases and statutes to analysis of the U. S. Constitution and Bill of Rights with case law annotations. A good place to begin legal research. The site contains extensive search features.

iCourthouse   http://www.icourthouse.com

iCourthouse is "The courthouse for the Internet." iCourthouse is a greatly stream-lined version of the court system in the real world. Cases here move at Internet speed. The cases are real, the jurors are real, and the verdicts are real. Collect your evidence and present your case. iCourthouse is always in session.

JOSHUA: The Florida Court System   http://www.flcourts.org

JOSHUA is a statewide information system serving Florida's Judiciary.

Law.com   http://www.law.com

An excellent site for lawyers, students, and business and government officials to learn more about the law. Plenty of legal resources, a legal dictionary, a careers service, and state-specific databases are available.

LawCrawler   http://www.lawcrawler.com

Search for keywords or by relevant Web sites.

Law Links   http://www.lawnewsnetwork.com/links

The links collection of the Law News Network. A great starting point for anyone doing legal research on the Web.

Lexis ONE   http://www.lexisone.com

An excellent free legal research site providing searchable case law, free legal forms, a statutory law guide, a legal Internet guide, and much more. The site is part of the Lexis-Nexis family of products.

The 'Lectric Law Library   http://www.lectlaw.com

A huge collection of legal reference materials and links.

Mega Law   http://www.megalaw.com

A rich resource that's useful as a starting point for Web-based legal research.

National Center for State Courts   http://www.ncsc.dni.us

Organization providing support and assistance to state courts and their operation.

U. S. Supreme Court Online   http://www.supremecourtus.gov

Round the clock access to the U. S. Supreme Court! This site provides public access to the Court's decisions, argument calendar, schedules, rules, visitors' guides, building photos, and bar admission forms. The site has decision texts available online by noon on the day they are announced (which always occurs at 10 A.M. ET).

Washburn University School of Law—WashLaw Web
http://www.washlaw.edu

A great collection of criminal justice- and law-related sites, with a good search feature.

WWW Virtual Law Library (Indiana University School of Law)
http://www.law.indiana.edu/v-lib

The World Wide Web Virtual Library is a collection of subject-related Web sites maintained by institutions throughout the world, each administering a different subject. The Law Library is one of those sites, and provides users with the ability to search for legal information on the Web. Users can also browse by category (such as "Criminal Law and Evidence").

Corrections Sites

Center for Rational Correctional Policy
http://pierce.simplenet.com/prisonerresources.html

This site contains general information on retributive sentencing and correctional policies. Includes corrections departments by state.

Corrections Connection   http://www.corrections.com

Voted a Microsoft "Outstanding Criminal Justice Site," the Corrections Connection provides links to almost any correctional organization in the country, and to all kinds of corrections information. The Corrections Connection contains over 10,000 links to corrections-related sites and literature.

Correctional Service of Canada   http://www.csc-scc.gc.ca

The Correctional Service of Canada seeks to make a positive difference in the lives of offenders and in the attitudes that govern their behavior.

Corrections (NCJRS)   http://www.ncjrs.org/corrhome.htm

This site is an extensive source of information on criminal and juvenile justice providing services to an international community of policymakers and professionals. NCJRS is a collection of clearinghouses supporting all bureaus of the U. S. Department of Justice.

Corrections Corporation of America
http://www.correctionscorp.com

Corrections Corporation of America (CCA) is the leading private sector provider of detention and corrections services to federal, state, and local governments. The company designs, constructs, finances, and manages new or existing facilities.

Federal Bureau of Prisons (BOP)
http://www.bop.gov

The BOP site provides various selections, including: Quick Facts and Statistics, Weekly Population Reports, Program Statements (Policies), Inmate Information, and Employment Information.

National Institute of Corrections (NIC)
http://www.bop.gov/nicpg/nicmain.html

NIC is an agency under the U. S. Department of Justice. It provides assistance to federal, state, and local corrections agencies working with adult offenders.

Prison Issues Desk   http://www.prisonactivist.org

The Prison Issues Desk is the source for progressive and radical information on prisons and the criminal prosecution system.

Prison Zone   http://www.prisonzone.com

Offers poetry, books, art, and writings by inmates.

U. S. Sentencing Commission   http://www.ussc.gov

The United States Sentencing Commission is an independent agency in the judicial branch of government charged with setting federal sentencing policy and standards.

Crime Prevention

Antistalking Web Site   http://www.antistalking.com

This is a site for anyone concerned about the crime of stalking. It is intended not only as a resource for stalking victims but as a site for law enforcement personnel, mental health professionals, researchers, educators, legislators, and security personnel.

Crime and Violence Prevention Center
http://caag.state.ca.us/cvpc

The site of the Crime and Violence Prevention Center in the California Attorney General's Office offers quality multimedia prevention materials dealing with child

FIGURE 3-3
The Partnerships Against Violence Network (PAVNET) home page
(http://www.pavnet.org). PAVNET is an excellent site for criminal justice
researchers and students interested in violence prevention.

abuse, drug abuse, gangs, domestic violence, school violence, violence, and general crime.

Crime Stoppers International (CSI)   http://www.c-s-i.org

This is the Web site of Crime Stoppers International. The site was established to support a worldwide network of Crime Stoppers programs, and to contribute to the development of Crime Stoppers as an effective crime-solving organization throughout the world.

Cybercrime.gov   http://www.cybercrime.gov

A Web site run by the Computer Crime and Intellectual Property Section of the U. S. Department of Justice, and dealing with all aspects of cybercrime.

Fraud Watch   http://www.fraud-watch.com

A service of Forensic Intelligence Display & Analysis, Inc., the Fraud-Watch site contains information about fraudulent medical disability claims detection, control, and litigation.

National Crime Prevention Council   http://www.ncpc.org

The Council offers crime prevention tips for self, home, and family; community policing; neighborhood building; and information on McGruff the Crime Dog and his nephew, Scruff. Find out how you can help "Take A Bite Out Of Crime!"

National Fraud Information Center   http://www.fraud.org

The goal of the Center is to fight the growing menace of telemarketing fraud by improving prevention and enforcement.

 Office of National Drug Control Policy (ONDCP)
http://www.whitehousedrugpolicy.gov

This agency serves as the central research and development organization within the U. S. government for counterdrug enforcement and drug abuse education, prevention, and treatment.

 Partnerships Against Violence (PAVNET)
http://www.pavnet.org

Partnerships Against Violence Network (PAVNET) is a "virtual library" of information about violence and at-risk youth, representing data from seven different federal agencies. Violence prevention professionals can communicate and share resources through the PAVNET mailgroup. NCJRS says that PAVNET is "A Model of Internet Use."

 Vera Institute of Justice   http://www.vera.org

Working in collaboration with government, the Vera Institute of Justice designs and implements innovative programs that encourage just practices in public services and improve the quality of urban life.

Forensics

 American Board of Criminalists
http://www.criminalistics.com/ABC

The American Board of Criminalists supports a peer-developed and peer-reviewed certification program for those working in the field of criminalistics.

Center for Forensics Studies   http://www.phys.ttu.edu/cfs

The Center for Forensic Studies at Texas Tech University was established in 1982 with the aim of promoting innovation in physical evidence examination.

CompuForensics   http://www.compuforensics.com

CompuForensics provides information on the skills needed for safely locating and securing evidence at a crime scene, as well as competently analyzing, decrypting, and/or restoring data at the CompuForensics facility.

Criminalistics-dot-Com   http://www.criminalistics.com

Home page of the American Board of Criminalistics, which provides a peer-developed and peer-reviewed certification program, based on assessment of competency using written examinations and proficiency testing.

Environmental Protection Agency's National Enforcement Investigations Center   http://es.epa.gov/oeca/oceft/neic

NEIC supports the environmental enforcement community through expertise in field activities and engineering evaluations, forensic laboratory activities, information management, computer forensics, technical analysis and training, and in the courtroom.

Evidence: The True Witness   http://library.thinkquest.org/17049

An award-winning student-created site about forensics. It's well worth a visit.

FBI Laboratory   http://www.fbi.gov/programs/lab/labhome.htm

The home page of the FBI's crime laboratory.

Firearms ID   http://www.firearmsID.com

This site provides an introduction to forensic firearms identification.

Forensic Art   http://www.forensicartist.com

A Web site dedicated to forensic art.

Forensic Dentistry   http://www.cincytoothdoc.com

This site contains lots of information about forensic dentistry along with case examples.

Forensic Entomologists World Wide
http://www.uio.no/~mostarke/forens_ent/forensic_entomologists.html

A directory consisting of names, e-mail addresses, WWW home pages, and other information about forensic entomologists all around the world.

Forensic Justice Project   http://www.forensicjustice.org

The Forensic Justice Project monitors the performance of the FBI crime lab with the avowed mission of ensuring justice through the use of forensic evidence.

Forensic Science Center
http://hyperion.advanced.org/17133/forindex.html

Includes information on explosives, forensic anthropology, ballistics, blood and body fluids, entomology, DNA, fingerprints, hair and fibers, photography, and more.

Forensic Science Resources (1)
http://www.lib.msu.edu/harris23/crimjust/forsci.htm

Forensic Science Reference Tools. The site has articles and related links.

Forensics Science Resources (2)
http://www.tncrimlaw.com/forensic

This site provides a bibliography suggested for anyone litigating forensic science evidence.

Kuglick's Forensic Resource and Criminal Law Search Site
http://www.kruglaw.com

Includes 1,500 forensic and criminal law links.

National Forensic Science Technology Center (NFSTC)
http://www.nfstc.org

NFSTC was established by the American Society of Crime Laboratory Directors in 1995 and began operating in July 1996. It is an independent not-for-profit organization.

Gangs

ATF Gang Resistance Education And Training Program (GREAT)   http://www.atf.treas.gov/great/great.htm

This site covers training related to the GREAT Program, a school-based gang prevention strategy taught to middle-school students.

Gang Information
http://www-bcf.usc.edu/~aalonso/Gangs/ganglinks.html

This site focuses on Los Angeles gangs, graffiti, and homicides.

Gang Prevention Incorporated
http://www.gangpreventioninc.com

The site focuses on street gang training provided by a Chicago law enforcement veteran with 15 years of experience who specializes in street gang identification, awareness, and activity. Three-day gang specialist certification classes are available as well as a 450-page gang identification manual.

Gangs in the Schools
http://eric-web.tc.columbia.edu/alerts/ia46.html

This site offers most of the gang-related documents and journal articles that have been entered into the Educational Resources Information Center (ERIC) database.

Gangs or Us   http://www.gangsorus.com

A Web site designed to help teachers, law enforcement and corrections personnel, as well as concerned citizens, in determining if street or prison gangs are operating in their community or corrections facility.

Koch Crime Commission   http://www.kci.org

Studying the criminal and juvenile justice system and identifying ways to reduce and prevent crime, especially juvenile crime.

National Youth Gang Center (NYGC)
http://www.iir.com/nygc

This site provides information about the NYGC Center. It collects and analyzes gang-related data on a nationwide basis, generating annual surveys and reports.

Streetgangs.com   http://www.streetgangs.com

The purpose of this site is to share research information about street gangs.

International Resources

Access to Justice Network Canada
http://www.acjnet.org/acjeng.html

Many links to information about the Canadian justice system.

Australasian Legal Information Institute
http://www.austlii.edu.au

Extensive collection of Australian legal materials, including cases, legislation, reports, and more. The site contains more than six gigabytes of raw text materials and over a million searchable documents.

Australian Institute of Criminology   http://www.aic.gov.au

This site offers a substantial online collection of research and reports dealing with crime and justice in Australia and the rest of the world.

Canadian Crime and Justice Statistics
http://www.statcan.ca/english/Pgdb/State/justic.htm

An extensive collection of data on crime and justice in Canada.

Canadian Criminal Justice Resource Page
http://members.tripod.com/~BlueThingy/index.html

Extensive links to Canadian criminal justice information.

Canadian Criminal Justice System
http://www.criminaldefence.com

Links to many resources dealing with Canadian law, courts, and corrections.

Canadian Department of Justice   http://canada.justice.gc.ca

Home page of the Canadian Department of Justice, the site also provides many links to Canadian legislative initiatives and crime and justice sites.

Chinalaw Web   http://www.qis.net/chinalaw

Chinalaw Web offers a wealth of information about Chinese law and the legal system in greater China, including Taiwan, Hong Kong, the People's Republic of China, and the Portuguese Colony of Macau.

European Institute for Crime Prevention and Control (HEUNI)
http://www.vn.fi/om/suomi/heuni

The European Institute for Crime Prevention and Control, affiliated with the United Nations (HEUNI) is the European link in the network of institutes operating within the framework of the United Nations Crime Prevention and Criminal Justice Program.

EUROPOL   http://www.europol.eu.int

The site of the European Police Office. Europol began operation in October 1998, and works to improve effectiveness and cooperation among member states in preventing and combating terrorism, unlawful drug trafficking, and other serious forms of international crime.

Home Office of the United Kingdom
http://www.homeoffice.gov.uk/rds/index.htm

Downloadable statistics about crime, criminal justice, and other data about the United Kingdom.

Osaka University (Japan) Faculty of Law Legal Resource List
http://www.law.osaka-u.ac.jp

A Japanese law-related resource guide to international crime and justice data, with links to more than 70 countries.

International Criminal Court Ratification Campaign
http://www.hrw.org/campaigns/icc/icc-main.htm

Offers press releases and commentaries on the proposed International Criminal Court.

INTERPOL—USNCB   http://www.usdoj.gov/usncb

The U. S. National Central Bureau (USNCB) serves as the American arm of INTERPOL. USNCB is part of the U. S. Department of Justice.

National Institute of Justice International Center
http://www.ojp.usdoj.gov/nij/international

Home page of NIJ's International Center. The Center was created in 1997 as a response to the increasing globalization of crime. The Center provides communities and jurisdictions in the United States and overseas with resources designed to assist practitioners, researchers, and policymakers meet new challenges. The International Center seeks to stimulate, facilitate, evaluate, and disseminate both national and international criminal justice research and information. A key feature of the site is the Center's fully searchable virtual library—a repository of information related to comparative, international, and transnational crime and justice issues.

Office of International Criminal Justice (OICJ)
http://www.oicj.org

OICJ works to improve the administration of criminal and juvenile justice both at home and abroad by providing enhanced opportunities for communication and collaboration by both academics and practitioners.

Police Services of the United Kingdom   http://www.police.uk
Official Web site of the U. K. police. Information is organized by area policed.

Royal Canadian Mounted Police (RCMP)
http://www.rcmp-grc.gc.ca

The Web site for the well-known Royal Canadian Mounted Police. This extensive site provides information on many of the facets of the RCMP.

The Russian Legal Server
http://solar.rtd.utk.edu/~sanor/main.html

Extensive online legal information about Russia.

Scandinavian Research Council for Criminology
http://rvik.ismennt.is/~tho/NSfK.html

Established in 1962 by ministries of Justice in Denmark, Finland, Iceland, Norway, and Sweden to further criminological research and advise Scandinavian governments, this site contains bibliographic information about the Council's publications.

Scotland Yard (United Kingdom)   http://www.met.police.uk

Official Web site of this prominent British criminal investigations agency. The site contains much information about the agency and its work.

Solicitor General of Canada   http://www.sgc.gc.ca

Web site of the office responsible for the prosecution of crime in Canada. Many links to crime and justice information.

United Nations Crime and Justice Information Network (UNCJIN)   http://www.uncjin.org

Creation of the United Nations Crime and Justice Information Network (UNCJIN) was mandated by United Nations Economic and Social Council resolution 1986/11. This electronic clearinghouse represents the culmination of several years of incremental efforts coordinated by the United Nations Center for International Crime Prevention, Vienna. From 1995 to 1999, UNCJIN was hosted and supported by the Institute of Applied Computer Science and Information Systems at the University of Vienna. A new version of UNCJIN is under construction as this book goes to press, and is being integrated into the United Nation's Office for Drug Control and Crime Prevention's Web site at http://www.odccp.org/crime_prevention.html.

United Nations Interregional Crime & Justice Research Institute (UNICRI)   http://www.unicri.it

Located in Rome, UNICRI was established in 1968 to strengthen the U. N.'s actions in the prevention and control of crime. The UNICRI Documentation Center contains an exhaustive library on the prevention and control of crime and deviance.

United Nations Online Crime and Justice Clearinghouse (UNOJUST)   http://www.ncjrs.org/unojust

The site provides a wealth of data about crime and criminal justice worldwide.

World Factbook of Criminal Justice Systems
http://www.ojp.usdoj.gov/bjs/abstract/wfcj.htm

This site provides a comprehensive full-text report detailing criminal justice systems worldwide.

World Justice Information Network (WJIN)
http://www.wjin.net

This site represents an experiment in building a global network of knowledge about crime and justice. It provides current international news and documents about transnational crime and justice for the international user. Apply for free membership in order to access the site's full features.

Justice Statistics

 ### Bureau of Justice Statistics (BJS)   http://www.ojp.usdoj.gov/bjs

The Bureau of Justice Statistics (BJS), a component of the Office of Justice Programs in the U. S. Department of Justice, is the primary source within the United States for criminal justice statistics.

 ### Death Penalty Information Center (DPIC)
http://www.deathpenaltyinfo.org

This site contains an extensive collection of information and statistics on and about the death penalty.

 ### Drug Enforcement Administration (DEA)
http://www.usdoj.gov/dea

The DEA's official home page. Lots of statistics and publications available, along with a history of the agency.

 ### Sourcebook of Criminal Justice Statistics
http://www.albany.edu/sourcebook

Home of the online version of the *Sourcebook of Criminal Justice Statistics*—the largest compilation of criminal justice statistics available anywhere. The Sourcebook site is run by the State University of New York at Albany, and is updated continuously.

The White House's Social Statistics Briefing Room
http://www.whitehouse.gov/fsbr/crime.html

Collection of selected data concerning crime in the United States.

 Uniform Crime Reports (UCR)   http://www.fbi.gov/ucr/ucr.htm

The most recent crime reports collected by the FBI and made available to the public. Historical data is also available.

Violence Against Women Office (VAWO) Research and Statistics   http://www.ojp.usdoj.gov/vawo/statistics.htm

This page contains collected research reports, projects, and statistical publications concerning crimes against women.

Juvenile Justice Sites

American Family Foundation   http://www.csj.org

Provides a wealth of information on the family—including information on cults and hate groups.

Child Quest International   http://www.childquest.org

An organization dedicated to finding missing children.

Children's Defense Fund   http://www.childrensdefense.org

One of the most influential children's advocacy groups.

 HandsNet—Building the Human Services Community Online
http://www.handsnet.org

Dedicated to bringing human services information online. Offers a time-saving Web clipping service for human services professionals.

 Juvenile Justice at NCJRS   http://www.ncjrs.org/jjhome.htm

Many links to full-text juvenile justice resources provided by the National Criminal Justice Reference Service.

The Juvenile Justice Clearinghouse
http://www.fsu.edu/~crimdo/jjclearinghouse

Maintains an extensive collection of juvenile justice related Web links.

The Juvenile Justice Home Page
http://home.earthlink.net/~ehumes/homejuv.htm

A collection of resources, links, and information on juvenile court and juvenile justice issues.

Juvenile Justice Magazine online
http://www.juvenilejustice.com

Current issues of this bi-monthly magazine are available.

Juvenile Law Center   http://www.jlc.org

Information on juvenile law for professionals and families. Frequently asked questions on delinquency, truancy, emancipation, and more.

National Council of Juvenile and Family Court Judges
http://www.ncjfcj.unr.edu

The National Council of Juvenile and Family Court Judges is composed of judges, referees, and commissioners who confront a variety of juvenile- and family-related issues during their tenure, including child abuse and neglect; substance and alcohol abuse; termination of parental rights; domestic relations matters; child support enforcement; adoption and foster care; and juvenile delinquency. Associate membership is open to court services personnel, police and probation officers, attorneys, and other professionals and volunteers in the field of juvenile justice.

National Council on Crime and Delinquency (NCCD)
http://www.nccd-crc.org

Web site of this research and advocacy group with annotated links to related sites. Focus of the group is on children as victims and perpetrators of crime and on needs of dependent children.

Office of Juvenile Justice and Delinquency Prevention
http://ojjdp.ncjrs.org

The OJJDP Web site is designed to provide information and resources on both general areas of interest about juvenile justice and delinquency—including conferences, funding opportunities, and new publications—and on the comprehensive strategy as a framework for communities to combat youth crime.

Outward Bound   http://www.outwardbound.org

Web site of organization that seeks to build character through a wilderness experience.

U. S. Department of Health and Human Services, Division of Children and Youth Policy
http://aspe.os.dhhs.gov/hsp/cyphome.htm

Law Enforcement Resources

911 Audio.com   http://www.911audio.com

Listen to fire, police, and other emergency broadcasts. The site also offers much 911-related information and contains a list of suggested sites for finding similar broadcasts elsewhere.

 Ira Wilsker's Law Enforcement Sites
http://www.ih2000.net/ira

Extensive collection of links to law enforcement sites. Particular focus on Southeast Texas, but the collection incorporates many other sites in the United States.

 Law Enforcement Links (LEOLINKS)   http://www.leolinks.com

Many links to law enforcement sites with a good search feature.

 Police Guide   http://www.policeguide.com

One of the largest police sites on the Internet. The site consists of 238 separate Web pages—and is growing.

 Police Scanner.com   http://www.policescanner.com/police.stm

Here you'll find the latest live audio-enabled police sites. Run by Yahoo! Broadcase, featured sites include the LAPD, NYPD, Dallas PD, San Diego PD, Dallas Sheriff's Office, Plano (Texas) PD, and the Miami PD.

Terrorism

 Counterterrorist Organization Profiles
http://www.terrorism.com/terrorism/CTgroups.html

Information about those who combat terrorism worldwide.

Extremistgroups.com (terrorism, hate groups)
http://www.extremistgroups.com

Extremistgroups.com publishes the book *Investigating Extremist Groups: A Manual and Resource Guide for Law Enforcement*. Its site also offers useful links for information on extremists as well as lists of the latest books about investigations and extremists.

Terrorism Documents
http://www.terrorism.com/terrorism/documents.html

Links to documents maintained by the Terrorism Research Center (see below).

 Terrorism Research Center   http://www.terrorism.com

Many online resources dealing with terrorism, terrorist organizations, and anti-terrorism efforts.

 Terrorist Group Profiles
http://www.terrorism.com/terrorism/Groups2.html

Profiles of terrorist groups maintained by the Terrorism Research Center.

U. S. Department of State: Countering Terrorism
http://www.usinfo.state.gov/topical/pol/terror

Official Web site of the U. S. Department of State dealing with current initiatives to combat global terrorism.

U. S. Department of State: Office of the Coordinator of Counterterrorism
http://www.state.gov/www/global/terrorism/index.html

Official U. S. government Web site with information and links dealing with counter-terrorism.

 U. S. Department of State: Patterns of Global Terrorism Reports (1994–1998)   http://www.hri.org/docs/USSD-Terror

Text of the State Department's analysis of global terrorism. Brief discussion of terrorist acts and organizations and discussion of anti-terrorist initiatives.

Unsolved Crimes

America's Most Wanted   http://www.amw.com

Web site of the popular television show.

Australia's Most Wanted
http://www.crimestoppers.net.au/wanted

Has information about the "top ten" most wanted in Australia.

Crime Scene Evidence Files   http://www.crimescene.com

An unusual site that has detailed information about various crimes around the United States. Visitors are invited to view the evidence and help "solve" the crime.

Cyber Criminals Most Wanted (cybercrime prevention)
http://www.ccmostwanted.com

First complete cybercrime prevention Web site on the net. Topics include security, safety, cyberstalking, viruses, hoaxes, scams. Special sections for kids, families, lawyers, policemen, seniors.

FBI's Top Ten Most Wanted Fugitives
http://www.fbi.gov/mostwant/topten/tenlist.htm

Official FBI site with information about their "top ten" most wanted. (Rewards up to $1 million.)

Fugitive Hunter's Top 100 Fugitives
http://www.digidezign.com/~fugitivehunter

Top 100 wanted fugitives.

Missing and Exploited Children's Program
http://www.ncjrs.org/ojjdp/missing

The Program coordinates activities to prevent abductions and the exploitation of children and to locate missing children; it also addresses the psychological impact of abduction.

National Crime Information Exchange
http://www.angelfire.com/nc/crimeinformation/index.html

Site with summary information about many unsolved crimes. The purpose is to obtain information that might help solve the crime. Also has numerous links to related sites and law enforcement.

World's Most Wanted: Fugitives and Unsolved Crimes
http://mostwanted.org

Private organization's most wanted list.

Victims of Crime

Center for Crime Victims' Rights, Remedies, and Resources
http://www.newhaven.edu/UNH/ShowcaseSites/CenterStudyCrimeVictims.html

The School of Public Safety and Professional Studies of the University of New Haven is the home for the Center for the Study of Crime Victims' Rights, Remedies, and Resources. The Center provides and develops numerous initiatives to assist crime victims through educational, training, and technical assistance opportunities. The center's goal is to serve the various academic disciplines and professional groups that study, advocate for, or serve victims.

International Victiminology Web Site (IVW)
http://www.victimology.nl/rechts.htm

Hosted by the Research and Documentation Center of the Netherlands Ministry of Justice in cooperation with the U. N. Center for International Crime Prevention and the World Society of Victimology.

 ### National Center for Victims of Crime (formerly the National Victim Center)   http://www.nvc.org

Extensive online resource for victim information and advocacy. Contains many links and information about the organization's advocacy efforts.

National Organization for Victim Assistance (NOVA)
http://www.try-nova.org

The National Organization for Victim Assistance is a private, non-profit organization of victim and witness assistance programs and practitioners, criminal justice agencies and professionals, mental health professionals, researchers, former victims and survivors, and others committed to the recognition and implementation of victim rights and services.

National Victims' Constitutional Amendment Network (NVCAN)   http://www.nvcan.org

NVCAN supports the adoption of a U. S. Constitutional amendment recognizing the fundamental rights of crime victims to be treated with dignity, fairness, and respect by the criminal justice system.

 ### Office for Victims of Crime (OVC)
http://www.ojp.usdoj.gov/ovc

U. S. Department of Justice site with information about crime victims and resources for crime victims. Contains an extensive collection of links to other relevant information.

 ### Parents of Murdered Children (POMC)   http://www.pomc.com
The National Organization of Parents of Murdered Children (POMC)® is the only national helping organization which is specifically for the survivors of homicide victims and which follows up with supportive family services after the murder of a family member or friend.

Victims' Information at NCJRS   http://ncjrs.org/victhome.htm

An extensive collection of information about victims of crime.

World Society of Victimology
http://www.world-society-victimology.de

Includes electronic access to the journal of the World Society of Victimology—*The Victimologist.*

Violence against Women

Battered Women's Support Services   http://www.bwss.org

Battered Women's Support Services offers information, referral, advocacy, and support to battered women.

Behind Closed Doors   http://home1.gte.net/llrother/closed.html

An artistic multimedia collaborative project that deals with issues of domestic violence and provides links to local support groups.

CAVNET   http://www.asksam.com/cavnet

Home to the Communities Against Violence Network.

Domestic Abuse Counseling Center   http://trfn.clpgh.org/dacc

A non-profit organization that offers assistance to victims of domestic violence and abuse.

Domestic Violence Information Center
http://www.feminist.org/other/dv/dvhome.html

A large collection of information and links dealing with violence against women.

Family Violence Research Program   http://www.unh.edu/frl

Web site devoted to understanding family violence and the impact of violence in families.

Lady Care   http://www.webruler.com/ladycare/Abuse.htm

This site offers awareness and insight into domestic violence/wife abuse by providing information, resources, statistics, and a personal story.

Los Angeles Commission on Assaults Against Women
http://www.lacaaw.org/home.html

Crisis counseling, teen abuse prevention, and more.

Men and Women against Domestic Violence
http://www.silcom.com/~paladin/madv

An Internet-based organization with many links and some information concerning domestic violence, its effects and treatment.

 ### National Domestic Violence Hotline   http://www.ndvh.org

The National Domestic Violence Hotline links individuals to help in their area using a nationwide database that includes detailed information on domestic violence shelters, other emergency shelters, legal advocacy and assistance programs, and social service programs. Available in both English and Spanish.

National Sexual Violence Resource Center (NSVRC)
http://www.nsvrc.org

The NSVRC, a project of the Pennsylvania Coalition Against Rape, has as its mission to (1) strengthen the support system serving sexual assault survivors by enhancing the capacity of sexual assault providers at the national, state, and community levels, (2) provide information and technical assistance to support effective interventions in preventing sexual violence, and (3) identify emerging policy issues and research needs to support the development of policy and practice specific to the intervention and prevention of sexual violence.

Reclaim the Night
http://www.vicnet.net.au/vicnet/reclaim/rtnight.htm

Web site of an Australian annual event "where thousands of women and children rally together to protest violence against women and children and to celebrate women's diversity, visibility, and strength."

Ritual Abuse   http://www.xroads.com/rahome/rahome.html

Provides information about ritualistic abuse and support for survivors.

Sexual Assault Information
http://www.cs.utk.edu/~bartley/saInfoPage.html

Extensive collection of links concerning sexual assault.

Violence against Women Office (VAWO)
http://www.ojp.usdoj.gov/vawo

U. S. Department of Justice office dealing with violence against women. The site includes information on what communities can do, grant information, statistics, and federal VAW laws and regulations.

USING THE WEB

Visit the following Justice Information Center and *Talk Justice* sites on the Web:

>> Justice Information Center: http://www.ncjrs.org
>> *Talk Justice:* http://talkjustice.com

Then do the following:

1. Write a page describing the features available at each of these sites. Compare the sites. What does NCJRS offer that *Talk Justice* doesn't? What are the major differences between the two?
2. Use the NCJRS site to research community policing. How many references can you find to community policing? How many full-text documents on the topic are available through the site? What other sites does NCJRS refer you to for additional community policing information?

E-Mail and E-Mail Software

More than one million e-mail messages pass through the Internet every hour.

—*Planet IT*[14]

I have received no more than one or two letters in my life that were worth the postage.

—*Henry David Thoreau*

I have made this letter longer than usual, only because I have not had the time to make it shorter.

—*Blaise Pascal*, Provincial Letters

CHAPTER OUTLINE

Introduction

Sending Messages

Receiving Messages

Emoticons and Abbreviations

Free E-Mail

Locator and Directory Services

E-Mail Security

Using the Web

INTRODUCTION

One of the most useful tools available to anyone on the Internet is electronic mail. Electronic mail is called **e-mail** for short. E-mail allows you to exchange messages with other Internet users. Almost all online services and Internet service providers assign you at least one e-mail address. Some, like America Online, provide as many as eight. Almost every Internet service provider makes e-mail available to its users. Hence, e-mail usually costs no more than you would normally pay to use your Internet service. You can send and receive any number of messages (although the size of messages is sometimes limited by your Internet provider's hardware and software) at any time of the day. Once you begin using e-mail for distant communication you will find that it is far cheaper than telephone calls![15]

In order to send and receive e-mail messages you must either be a member of an online service (in which case your e-mail capabilities are likely to be integrated with the software you received) or have special e-mail software loaded on your computer. You will need e-mail software if you are connecting to the Internet via an Internet service provider. Today's most popular e-mail programs are Netscape Mail (formerly called Netscape Messenger®), which is prepackaged as a component of Netscape Communicator®; Microsoft's Outlook® or Outlook Express®; and Eudora® (which also comes in a Pro version) by Qualcomm Corporation. As of this writing, all three of these e-mail programs are free. The most powerful, in terms of the number of options it offers, is probably Eudora—but only in its nonfree professional version, Eudora Pro®. A freeware version of Eudora® (see Figure 4-1), is available from Qualcomm Corporation at http://www.eudora.com.

> **E-Mail:** electronic mail. A modern form of communication utilizing computers and the Internet.

E-mail software not only allows you to send messages across the Internet, but most of today's e-mail programs make it possible for you to incorporate color images, audio, and even motion and video into your e-mail messages. You can send talking e-mail by recording your voice and embedding it in your e-mail message before sending (Eudora can be set to read the titles of your messages to you as mail arrives in your inbox). You can also include a photo or video of yourself as you speak—making for a true multimedia experience for your message recipients! The truly adventurous can use cutting-edge technology like LifeFX's Facemail software, which uses an animated human face to speak the entire contents of mail messages. A variety of virtual personalities and physical appearances are available for selection. Facemail is free at http://www.facemail.com or http://www.lifefx.com, but requires that both the mail sender and recipient have the Facemail software installed on their machines.

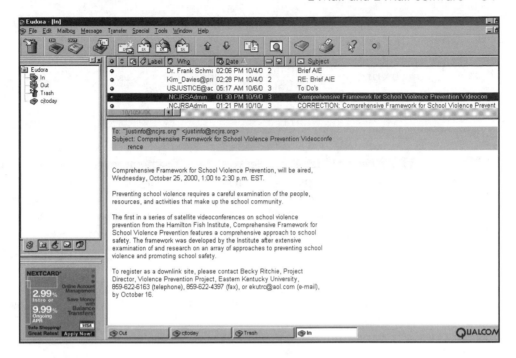

FIGURE 4-1

The Eudora (freeware) e-mail program. The inbox is displaying a message from JUSTINFO at NCJRS.

Keep in mind, however, that features like Facemail, embedded images and sound files, and fancy backgrounds and text, are recent innovations and have not always been a part of e-mail. Like Facemail, many advanced e-mail features require that your e-mail recipients have the technology (both hardware and software) to electronically decipher the messages you send and to display all of the enhancements you have included. Remember that if you get too far out on the leading edge of e-mail technology, only relatively few people may possess the technology needed to read (or to see and hear) your messages.

SENDING MESSAGES

Perhaps the best way to begin working with any e-mail software (short of reading the manual) is to create an outgoing message. An outgoing message is one that you send to someone else. Each mail program is a bit different. In order to compose a new message in Outlook Express, you need to click on the "New Mail" icon on the upper left side of the toolbar. In Outlook, click on "New" in the same location on the toolbar. Clicking on these icons opens a composition window, allowing you to type in the message you want to send.

After typing your message in the **composition field**, address the message. Do this by entering the name of the recipient in the TO field. E-mail addresses take the form of username@domainname. If you wanted to write to the Webmaster at the *Talk Justice* site, for example, you would address your message to admin@talkjustice.com. You can also send e-mail to a member of an online service. If you wanted to write to one of the many addresses used by the Justice Research Association, for example, you might send mail to usjustice@aol.com. In this case, the "aol.com" portion of the address refers to an e-mail box residing on America Online. If you are using an online service and want to send mail to someone on the same service (AOL, for example), you need only to type the name of the intended recipient in the "TO" box. Thus, for the example just given, if you were an AOL member and were to use the built-in mail service, you would simply type the username "usjustice" without specifying the domain (aol.com). If you inadvertently typed in the complete address, including the domain name, your online service should still properly interpret the address and send your mail to the correct recipient.

Keep in mind that you can always send the same message to more than one recipient. You can have a number of "TOs," or you can designate "cc" (carbon copy) recipients, and you can use "bcc" (blank carbon copy) to send mail to someone other than the main recipient without showing the recipient who else your message was sent to.

All e-mail programs contain an **address book**. Some e-mail programs even offer to add all addresses from the messages you receive to your address book (that can be a bad idea, especially if you receive a lot of unwanted mail). It is a good idea to keep addresses of frequent mail recipients in your address book. When you want to send mail, you can simply open the address book and click on the name of your intended recipient. The "TO" field will automatically be filled in with that person's e-mail address. Similarly, when you begin to type a person's name (or nickname, which you can also assign) into the "TO" field, your e-mail software will check your address book in order to determine if an entry exists for that person. If so, it will automatically fill in the "TO" field for you. (You can, of course, overwrite the "TO" entry manually if the address book selects the wrong recipient.)

It is always a good idea to fill in the **subject** field of the message you are sending. You might enter some brief text indicating what the message is about. If you are writing about the death penalty, for example, you might enter "Death penalty comments" or something similar.

Today's e-mail programs allow you to attach other kinds of files that you want to send to the addressee. A **file attachment** is simply a file attached to your e-mail message. When the message arrives in the recipient's e-mail box, he or she will see that the message contains an attachment. Attachments can be saved on a computer for later use or viewing, or you can double-click on most attachments (which may appear as a folder or file icon within the e-mail message) and open or run the file immediately. If you are sending proprietary forms of information such as recorded sound or video, make sure that the recipient has the necessary software on his or her computer to interpret or play such attachments.

Most programs also allow you to set a priority that will be associated with your message when it appears in the recipient's e-mail box. In order to do so from within the "New Message" window of Outlook Express (which will open after your click on "New Mail"), click on the "priority" selection in the toolbar. Eudora allows you to set message priority by clicking on the down arrow next to the small box containing a gray diamond shape that appears in the upper left-hand corner of your composition window.

You can also include a predefined **signature** in your e-mail messages. Outlook Express allows you to create a signature card and attach it to all of your messages. Recipients can conveniently drag the card into Windows Notepad® or Cardfile® and save it on their computer. Netscape Mail allows you to predefine a signature block to be attached to all messages—or to specify a file to be used as your signature. You can, for example, create a simple plain text (ASCII) file for Netscape to insert at the end of any messages you send. Most programs, including Eudora, give you the choice of whether to include a signature with a message you are about to send and then allow you to specify a choice from among a number of predefined signature blocks (or files).

After you have finished typing your message, you can send it. The button you need to click on varies slightly from program to program. If you are using Outlook Express, click on the little envelope icon on the left of the icon bar. Anyone using Netscape Mail will need to click on the round "send" button that shows a tilted envelope. Eudora users should click the "send" button as well.

If you decide not to send a message right away, you can save it for later editing. In order to open the message later, it will be necessary for you to locate the message in your "unsent messages," "drafts," or "saved messages" folder (depending on the software you are using) and click on it.

RECEIVING MESSAGES

When someone sends you a message, it is stored on the mail server of your online service or Internet service provider. In order to retrieve messages addressed to you, you must tell your mail program to check the mail server for your messages. Outlook requires you to click on "send and receive." Netscape Mail (see Figure 4-2) wants you to click on "Get Msg". And Eudora provides you with a small envelope topped by a down arrow, which stands for "download mail." Most mail programs

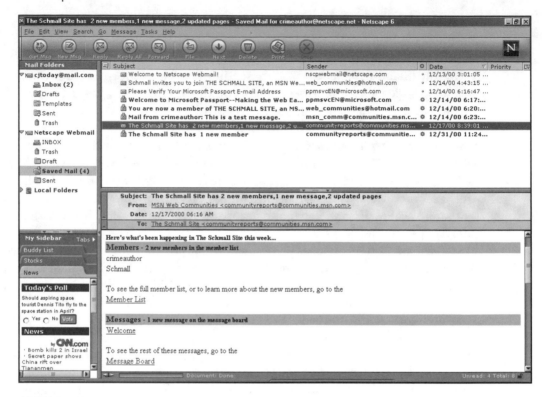

FIGURE 4-2

Netscape Communicator's e-mail screen.

Netscape Communicator browser window. © 1999 Netscape Communications Corporation. Used with permission. Netscape Communications has not authorized, sponsored, endorsed, or approved this publication and is not responsible for its content.

will also automatically check to see if you have mail. In order to enable this feature, however, you may have to click on "preferences" or "options" from within one of the pull-down menus on the menu bar.

You can set your e-mail program to store messages for you on the mail server even after you've read them. Alternatively, you can store mail that you have received on your own machine. If you are working in a network environment, all messages might be stored on a central server (which is not necessarily the same thing as a mail server) under your username. Generally, it is a good idea not to store messages on the mail server. Use your own machine for storage. Doing so will save a considerable amount of disk space on the mail server (especially if all users do the same thing). Moreover, most mail servers will delete mail you have read (and, sometimes, even mail you haven't read!) after a set period of time (30 or 90 days, for example).

When you receive a message you have a number of options. You can read the message and close it, allowing it to remain stored on the hard disk of your machine. You can decide not to read the message, and it will be saved automatically for your later use. You can file the message in a mail folder that you designate, you can print it (in which case it will remain visible on your screen until you take some other action), or you can delete it.

You can delete a message or a series of messages that you have selected with your mouse simply by clicking "delete" in most mail programs. Eudora, being a bit different, requires you to click on the trash can icon in order to delete the message. It is important to know that deleted messages are still saved by most e-mail programs in a special "trash" folder. You generally have to click on a menu option titled "empty trash" (or something similar) in order to permanently delete a message. Eudora, however, treats deleted messages a bit differently. All messages stored in Eudora's Trash mailbox are automatically deleted when you quit Eudora (although you can turn off this option).

You can, of course, choose to reply to mail that you receive. If you click on "reply" in Outlook (see Figure 4-3) and Netscape Mail or click the little envelope in Eudora's icon toolbar that has the blue arrow pointing to the left by it, you can reply to the person who sent you the message. If you want to send a message to

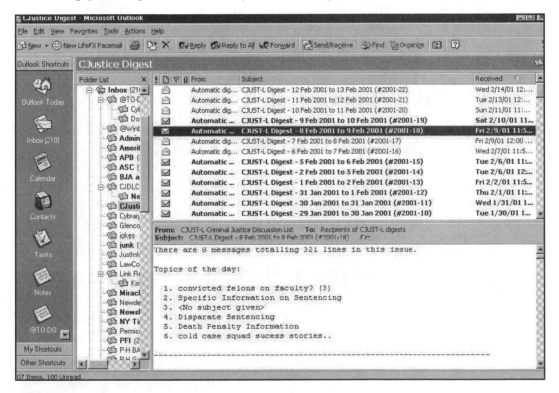

FIGURE 4-3
The Microsoft Outlook e-mail program. The user is viewing a folder containing messages from the CJUST-L e-mail discussion list.

everyone to whom the message was originally addressed, click on "reply to all." Often you can reply only to the sender because you may have been the only recipient. Once you click "reply," you will see the same window that is used to originate a message you want to send. In this case, however, the recipient's "TO" address will already be filled in, and the subject line will change to something like [RE: Death penalty comments]. Although you can change the subject line, your e-mail program is trying to be helpful by indicating which message you are replying to.

You can also forward e-mail by clicking on the "forward" icon or menu selection. If you choose to forward mail, you will need to fill in the address of the person(s) to whom you wish to forward the message. You need not type anything in the composition field that appears unless you wish to do so. If you type a message into the composition field of a message addressed to a forwarded address, the person to whom you are sending mail will receive your comments, followed by the message you are forwarding. Don't worry if the message you are about to forward doesn't appear in the composition field. Your e-mail program will still forward the message correctly.

Most e-mail programs save copies of messages that you have sent, enabling you to search or reread those messages at a later date. Your "sent" message folder usually contains such messages. The search feature built into most e-mail programs can prove to be a handy feature after you have sent a lot of messages and wish to find a particular one!

EMOTICONS AND ABBREVIATIONS

Today's e-mail programs have advanced far beyond early software that could deliver only text messages. Even so, the use of emoticons is still widespread. Emoticons are icons that express emotion. They are formed by a combination of keystroke characters that form a facial (or other) expression. Since people who read your e-mail messages cannot hear your voice, they can't tell whether you are trying to be funny, sarcastic, or serious. When you are kidding around, it is a good idea to include emoticons in your mail so that people don't take you too seriously. Emoticons are also called *smileys*, since the most common form of emoticon used on the Web is a smiling (or laughing) face. Common smileys, along with their translations, include the following:

:-) or :^) or :)	"I'm laughing." These are the basic smileys, used to inflect a sarcastic or joking tone into the writer's message.
|-)	More laughter (eyes closed).
:-(or : -(or :(	"I'm crying." "I'm sad." The boo-hoo smiley.
:-o	"Oops!" or "Uh-oh!"
;-)	"I just made a flirtatious and/or sarcastic remark." This kind of smiley is called a *winky*.

:-	"That was kind of devilish."
(-:	Laughter from a left-handed writer.
:-(	"I've been flamed."

While smileys add personality to your messages, abbreviations save keystrokes. Some common ones include the following:

BFN	Bye for now
BTW	By the way
G	Grin
GGG	Really big grin
HTH	Hope this helps
IJWTK	I just want to know
IJWTS	I just want to say
IMO	In my opinion
IMHO	In my humble opinion
LOL	Laughing out loud
OTOH	On the other hand
ROTFL	Rolling on the floor laughing
YMMV	Your mileage may vary

Sometimes, but not always, e-mail abbreviations are enclosed in pointed brackets (e.g., <LOL> or <GGG>).

FREE E-MAIL

A number of sites on the Internet offer free e-mail addresses. Some provide an e-mail box that you can use, personalized with a username and password of your choosing. Others, like BigFoot.Com, allow you to register a username "for life." Remember, however, that most free e-mail services must be accessed through your Web browser, and do not support stand-alone e-mail programs (like Outlook, Netscape Mail, and Eudora).

Bigfoot is a unique kind of service. It doesn't provide you with an e-mail box in the traditional sense, but rather forwards your mail to any e-mail address that you specify. Let's say that you set up a Bigfoot e-mail account with the username "bigdaddy." You could give anyone anywhere your Bigfoot e-mail address, which would be bigdaddy@bigfoot.com. Then, if you change service providers or online services, all you need to do is to tell Bigfoot where to send your mail. Keep in mind that to use Bigfoot you need to have existing e-mail service. Bigfoot's advantage lies in the fact that you can move, change e-mail addresses as often as you like, and still get all of your mail sent to your Bigfoot address at any time—even if people don't know which online service or ISP you are using.

You can get a Bigfoot e-mail address free. (The Justice Research Association's Bigfoot address is usjustice@bigfoot.com.) Bigfoot will then forward all mail sent to your "Bigfoot for life" address to one genuine e-mail account. Bigfoot allows you to have a copy of all your e-mail forwarded to up to five e-mail accounts. Bigfoot also provides filtering services, which allow you to have your incoming e-mail delivered or rejected based on criteria that you specify. If, for example, someone keeps flaming you with personal mail or repeatedly sends junk mail you don't want, you can tell Bigfoot to filter out mail from that individual.

Some of the best Bigfoot features are available as premium services for which you pay a small yearly fee. Bigfoot premium services include the following: (1) consolidation (where Bigfoot will consolidate messages from multiple e-mail accounts to one address of your choosing); (2) an e-mail reminder service where you can set up reminders to yourself for holidays, birthdays, and so forth; (3) a security feature, which you can use to have your incoming messages and attachments automatically filtered for viruses and other security threats; (4) an automatic reminder feature, which will automatically respond to incoming e-mail messages while you're away.

Other free e-mail services are available through many of the major search engines (discussed in Chapter 9). Some of them, like Bigfoot, provide "e-mail for life" addresses. As you surf the Web, you are likely to come across many advertisements for these free services.

According to CNet (http://www.cnet.com), a Web content provider that provides reviews of hardware, software, and Web services, the following are the best of these free Web-based e-mail services.

Yahoo! Mail   http://mail.yahoo.com

This is Cnet's first choice for Web-based free e-mail. If you visit the Yahoo! home page, click on "Yahoo! Mail" to sign up. After registering, you'll get an address like "schmalleger@yahoo.com. Yahoo! Mail offers free instant notification when new messages arrive via Yahoo! Messenger.

Microsoft's Hotmail   http://hotmail.com

MSN Hotmail integrates seamlessly with the MSN Explorer browser, and with Outlook and Outlook Express. It is also available using other browsers, and it offers good filters for eliminating junk mail.

Juno WebMail   http://webmail.juno.com

Unlike most other free Web-based e-mail services, Juno WebMail requires you to download and install software on your computer.

Mail.com   http://mail.com

Although CNET ranks Mail.com below the other major free services because it lacks some features, Mail.com does allow you to select from an interesting assortment of domain names. You can receive mail at addresses like "yourname@sociol-ogist.com", "yourname@teacher.com", "yourname@lawyer.com," and much more!

If you want a professional sounding e-mail address you might consider sign-ing up for free Web-based e-mail at places like law.com (which will provide you with an address like "yourname@law.com") or Justice Mail ("yourname@justice.com"). Justice Mail is a free service of FindLaw (http://www.findlaw.com).

Netscape WebMail (which you can reach via http://netscape.com), and Eudora WebMail (http://www.eudoramail.com) also offer high-quality free mail services, as do many of the search engines discussed in Chapter 6.

LOCATOR AND DIRECTORY SERVICES

What's Bill Gates's e-mail address? It's billg@microsoft.com. Are we breaching a confidence by telling you this? No, Bill's address is listed in most white-pages information directories on the Web. In fact, he has many addresses. We got this one by searching Yahoo!'s People Finder (http://people.yahoo.com). People Finder identifies the holder of this address as "Bill Gates: Microsoft Founder." If you want to see a picture of Mr. Gates, try another e-mail address search service at http://www.cs.indiana.edu/finger/gateway. Go to the site, enter:

billg@microsoft.com, and hit the return key.

If you want to find the e-mail addresses of friends, relatives, or almost any-one, try searching the following directory services:

Bigfoot   http://www.bigfoot.com

Bigfoot provides a mail directory locator service for the many people and busi-nesses it has registered online.

The Internet Address Finder (IAF)   http://www.iaf.net

Promotes itself as "the Internet's fastest and most convenient white pages service." Contains almost 7 million listings.

Yahoo! People Search   http://people.yahoo.com

People Search claims to be the world's number one people finder. Its slogan is "find anyone!"

Switchboard   http://www.switchboard.com

A comprehensive (and very good!) people locator.

WhoWhere?   http://www.whowhere.com

Find e-mail addresses, phone numbers, and street addresses of almost anyone on the Web with this comprehensive directory.

The World E-Mail Directory   http://www.worldemail.com

Over 18 million e-mail addresses and more than 140 million phone numbers at your fingertips.

Keep in mind that if you have an e-mail address, you can add it to any of these directories. You will, however, have to visit them to find out how.

You should also be aware of the best site on the Web for learning anything you ever wanted to know about e-mail. The site, "Mary Houten-Kemp's EveryThing E-Mail," includes (1) e-mail tips, (2) an e-mail glossary, (3) a list of mailing list discussion groups, (4) information on starting a mailing list, (5) a how-to guide on finding e-mail addresses, (6) a discussion of autoresponder services, (7) information on how to receive news by e-mail, (8) a discussion of unsolicited e-mail issues, and (9) links to free e-mail software. Mary Houten-Kemp's "EveryThing E-Mail" can be reached at http://everythingemail.net. The Houten-Kemp site is in the process of moving and changing its name. You will soon find the new site, "All About E-mail," at http://www.allaboutemail.com.

E-MAIL SECURITY

E-mail conversation is far from private. Other forms of electronic communication, including telephone calls and fax transmissions, are protected under a number of laws such as the Electronic Communications Privacy Act of 1986. Unfortunately for e-mailers, framers of the 1986 statute did not include most computer communications under the law.

E-mail security is difficult to ensure because e-mail messages are usually transferred from one computer to another as they make their way along the Internet to their final destinations. At each stop, almost any message can be intercepted and read by prying eyes. Why would someone want to read your e-mail? Hackers love the challenge of eavesdropping in cyberspace. Business competitors, on the other hand, can use what should be confidential information against you or your company. Remember that information, especially in today's world, is power.

Your company may feel that an employer has a right to read any e-mail you send using its system. Some companies appear to believe that reading an employee's e-mail is more than a right—it is a responsibility. Employers reason that

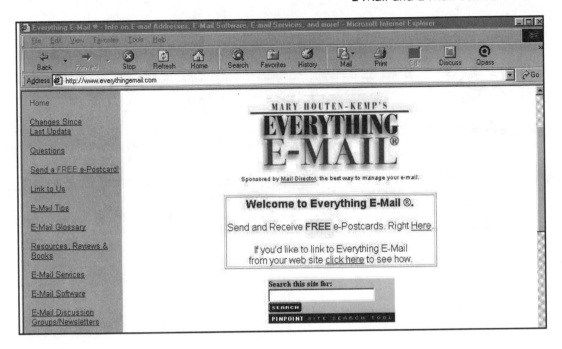

FIGURE 4-4

The home page of Mary Houten-Kemp's Everything E-Mail. The site offers e-mail tips, an e-mail glossary, links to free e-mail, and much more.
Copyright © 2001 by Everything E-Mail, http://www.everythingemail.com. Reprinted with permission.

employees should not be using the company's computers to send personal mail and that employees should not be wasting time at work doing so. High-technology companies often assert the right to read any mail sent over their computers as a precaution against industrial sabotage.

Universities are in a position similar to that of industrial corporations. Although most do not read student/faculty e-mail as a matter of policy, the possibility remains that they could do so if they wanted to. It is certainly better for any e-mail sender to be safe rather than sorry.

Remember a couple of personal protection rules when sending e-mail: (1) Don't send anything via e-mail that you wouldn't want anyone other than the intended recipient to see. (2) Use e-mail encryption techniques whenever you are sending sensitive information. (Security issues will be discussed at greater length in Chapter 9.)

USING THE WEB

Visit some of the free e-mail and directory services sites described in this chapter. Then do the following:

1. Compare at least three free e-mail sites. What features does each offer? What are the limitations of each site? Which do you like best? Why?

2. Use a few of the directory sites listed in this chapter to locate some of your friends or family members. Which directory site seems to be the best? Why?

5

E-Mail Discussion Lists, Newsgroups, 'Zines, and E-Journals

One thing on the Net is certain: there is always someone willing to argue about anything!

—*Anonymous*

There is no pleasure to me without communication: there is not so much as a sprightly thought comes into my mind that it does not grieve me to have produced alone, and that I have no one to tell it to.

—*Michel de Montaigne (1533–92), French writer[16]*

CHAPTER OUTLINE

INTRODUCTION

The quotation from the sixteenth-century French essayist, Michel de Montaigne, which begins this chapter, highlights the importance of interpersonal communication for the human soul. It seems that we, as human beings, have an innate need to share our thoughts and to tell others how we feel. The Internet provides a perfect medium for interpersonal communication, as it expands exponentially the number of people we are able to reach.

Communication on the Internet takes many forms. This chapter describes four: (1) e-mail discussion lists, (2) Internet newsgroups, (3) electronic journals, and (4) Internet-based magazines (called 'Zines). Each constitutes a form of communication not available a mere decade or so ago, and each is quite different from the others. We will discuss all four.

E-MAIL DISCUSSION LISTS

An e-mail **discussion list** sends e-mail messages from anyone participating in the list to all members of the list simultaneously. E-mail discussion lists work through a **listserver** (or **listserv**), which accepts e-mail contributions from group members and then redistributes them to all other members. In other words, when someone sends out a message, it goes to everybody on the list. Messages received by the listserver are sent to list members as soon as they arrive. Once a message has been sent, however, it is no longer available online.[17] Hence, if a new member joins an e-mail discussion list, he or she cannot access previous messages that were sent to the list.

> **Listserv:** a mailing list program that copies and distributes electronic mail to everyone subscribed to a particular e-mail discussion list.
>
> **Listserver:** a computer on which a listserv program runs.

A discussion list requires nothing other than an Internet connection and e-mail software. You must join the list, however, before you can participate. To subscribe, send a message to the listserver telling it to add you to the list. You will most likely need to send a message that takes the following form:

> subscribe listname yourfirstname yourlastname

In this example, the SUBSCRIBE command is followed by the name of the list you want to subscribe to, which is in turn followed by your name. Sometimes (depending on the list you are subscribing to) it is not necessary to type your name. By typing SUBSCRIBE you are giving the listserver a command to add you to the list. No punctuation is needed, and the command can generally be in lowercase or in capital letters.

When you send a command to the listserver, it is a good idea to delete your signature block (if one is automatically inserted into your e-mail messages), since the listserver will attempt to interpret the words it contains as commands. The listserver may respond by filling up your e-mail box with messages telling you that it doesn't understand what you are telling it to do.

The subscription process can vary widely from list to list. Joining some lists is accomplished simply by sending e-mail to the list moderator requesting list membership. The moderator will then issue the necessary commands to the listserver to add you to the list.

Keep in mind that two addresses are associated with any discussion list: (1) the address for the listserver, which is administrative and is used only for commands (such as SUBSCRIBE) and not for messages that you may want to send to the entire list, and (2) the discussion list address, to which messages intended for list members are sent. CJUST-L, the Criminal Justice Discussion List, for example, has a listserver address of LISTSERV@LISTSERV.CUNY.EDU, while messages are sent to list members at CJUST-L@LISTSERV.CUNY.EDU.

When you join a list, the first message you receive will be generated automatically by the listserver. It will cover administrative details, such as listserv commands for working with the list, and provide important information, such as the e-mail address that you will need to use to send messages to the discussion group. *Save this message.* If you ever want to leave the list (a process called unsubscribing), you will have to refer to it in order to know what command to use to sign off! If you don't know how to properly sign off of a list, you run the danger of receiving loads of unwanted e-mail for a very long time.

There are four types of lists: (1) announcement lists in which you receive messages but cannot post to the list, (2) discussion lists in which everyone on the list can participate in the discussion, (3) moderated lists, in which a list owner or moderator may review messages before they are sent to other members (moderators sometimes delete obscene messages and flames, keeping them from being passed along to list members, although they may make other kinds of decisions, as well), and (4) closed lists, which accept only members who meet certain criteria. The Police Discussion List, for example, is a closed list available only to active or retired law enforcement officers.

Once you join a discussion group, you do not have to actively participate in it by sending messages or by replying to other posts. If you prefer, you can stay in the background, reading messages that are of interest to you and assuming the status of a lurker on the list. You may find, however, that the list is sending you 50 or 100 messages a day or more! If you join more than one list, you can easily be overwhelmed by the sheer quantity of mail you receive.

In order to better manage mail received from listservers, you may want to use mail filter features built into your e-mail software. Filter options allow you to create special folders for each discussion list to which you belong and then route incoming mail from a list into a folder that you specify. You can also consolidate all messages from each discussion list using the DIGEST command. The DIGEST command tells the listserver to send you only one message each day containing all of the list's postings for that day. If you want to learn more about listserv commands, visit the L-Soft site at http://www.lsoft.com/listserv.stm. L-Soft originated much of the software that runs today's listservers. L-Soft software provides the basis for nearly 200,000 Internet e-mail discussion lists with over 82 million members. In a typical day nearly 60 million messages are delivered using L-Soft's software.

The next three sections provide a roster of criminology and criminal justice lists of both the announcement and discussion variety, followed by a catalog of discussion list resources. Included are instructions for joining (if you wish to join a "members only" list, you can always send a request to join to the list administrator asking for permission to join). Space permits printing only a small number of lists. For a more complete list of crime and justice discussion lists visit Florida State University's Criminal Justice Links page describing online discussion groups at http://www.fsu.edu/~crim/listserv.html.

Criminology and Criminal Justice Discussion Lists

Amnesty International
To subscribe send e-mail to listserv@suvm.syr.edu
In the body of the message type: subscribe AMNESTY *yourfirstname yourlastname*

The Australian Criminal Justice and Criminology Mailing List
To subscribe send e-mail to listserv@sulaw.law.su.oz.au
In the body of the message type: subscribe CRIM-L *yourfirstname yourlastname*

Corrections Discussion List
To subscribe visit http://groups.yahoo.com/group/Corrections and click "Join This Group."

Crime and Criminology (crime and criminology discussion forum)
To subscribe visit
http://groups.yahoo.com/group/crime_and_criminology and click "Join This Group."

Crime Books (true crime and crime fiction forum)
To subscribe visit http://groups.yahoo.com/group/crimebooks and click on "Join This Group."

Crime Writers
To subscribe visit http://groups.yahoo.com/group/crimewriters and click on "Join This Group."

Criminal Investigations   (for licensed investigators, law enforcement personnel and attorneys only)
To subscribe visit http://groups.yahoo.com/group/criminalinvestigations and click on "Join This Group."

Criminal Justice Alliance
To subscribe visit http://groups.yahoo.com/group/criminaljusticealliance and click on "Join This Group."

Criminal Justice Students
To subscribe visit http://groups.yahoo.com/group/CJstudents and click on "Join This Group."

Criminal Justice Studies
To subscribe visit http://groups.yahoo.com/group/cjs and click on "Join This Group."

Criminal Justice Discussion List
To subscribe send e-mail to LISTSERV@LISTSERV.CUNY.EDU
In the body of the message type: SUBSCRIBE CJUST-L *yourfirstname yourlastname*

The Criminal Justice Discussion List also provides an HTML based user interface at http://listserv.cuny.edu/archives/cjust-l.html. Use the interface to read archived messages, to subscribe and unsubscribe, and to view a description of the list. Another interface is available through Topica.com at http://www.topica.com/lists/cjust-l@cunyvm.cuny.edu.

Criminal Minds (for anyone interested in true crime, forensics, criminal profiling, etc.)
To subscribe visit http://groups.yahoo.com/group/criminalminds and click on "Join This Group."

Criminal Profiling
To subscribe visit http://groups.yahoo.com/group/Criminal_Profiling and click on "Join This Group."

Criminology Discussion List
To subscribe send e-mail to listserve@listserv.gmd.de
In the body of the message type: SUBSCRIBE CRIMINOLOGY

Critical Discussion of Crime, Society, and the Politics of Punishment List
To subscribe send e-mail to listproc@weber.ucsd.edu
In the body of the message type: subscribe CSPPLIST-L *yourfirstname yourlastname*

The Firearms-Politics List
To subscribe send e-mail to firearms-politics-request@tut.cis.ohio-state.edu
In the body of the message type: subscribe FIREARMS-POLITICS *yourfirstname yourlastname*

Forensic Psychology List
To subscribe visit http://groups.yahoo.com/group/forensicpsych and click on "Join This Group!"

Forensics Discussion List
To subscribe send e-mail to FORENS-REQUEST@ACC.FAU.EDU
In the body of the message type: subscribe FORENS-L *yourfirstname yourlastname*

International Criminal Court Information List
To subscribe visit http://groups.yahoo.com/group/icc-info and click on "Join This Group."

Internet Crime-L (a forum for individuals with an active role in the investigation and prosecution of crimes involving the Internet)
To subscribe visit http://groups.yahoo.com/group/InternetCrime-L and click on "Join This Group."

List guidelines and additional subscription instructions can be viewed at http://www.corpus-delicti.com/internetcrime-l.html

Journal of Criminal Justice and Popular Culture Discussion List

To subscribe send e-mail to listserv@listserv.albany.edu
In the body of the message type: subscribe CJMOVIES

A Web archive interface for the list can be found at http://listserv.albany.edu:8080/archives/cjmovies.html and also at http://www.topica.com/lists/cjmovies@cnsibm.albany.edu

The Justice Information Network Community Update

To subscribe send e-mail to listserv@listserv.wa.gov
In the body of the message type: SUBSCRIBE JIN-COMMUNITY-UPDATE

A Web archive interface for the list can be found at http://listserv.wa.gov/archives/jin-community-update.html

La Cosa Nostra (discuss the Italian Mafia)

To subscribe visit http://groups.yahoo.com/group/La_Cosa_Nostra and click "Join This Group!"

Law Enforcement Officers (for sworn law enforcement officers only)

To subscribe visit http://groups.yahoo.com/group/LEofficer and click on "Join This Group."

In order to become a member, you must fax a copy of your departmental credentials and a letter requesting that you be added to the list to Commander Chris Wagoner, the list moderator, at 352-334-0329. Include a telephone number in case verification is needed.

The National Crime Survey Discussion List

To subscribe send an e-mail to listserv@umdd.umd.edu
In the body of the message type: subscribe NCS-L *yourfirstname yourlastname*

The Police Discussion List (for sworn police officers)

To subscribe send e-mail to listserv@cunyvm.cuny.edu
In the body of the message type: subscribe POLICE-L *yourfirstname yourlastname*

Police Talk (for anyone interested in law enforcement issues)

To subscribe visit http://groups.yahoo.com/group/Police-Talk and click on "Join This Group."

The Victim's Assistance List

To subscribe send e-mail to listserv@pdomain.uwindsor.ca
In the body of the message type: subscribe VICTIM-ASSISTANCE *yourfirstname yourlastname*

Theoretical Criminology

To subscribe send e-mail to listserv@scas.sagepub.co.uk
In the body of the message type: SUBSCRIBE TCR-L
A Web archive interface for the list can be found at
http://www.sagepub.co.uk/archives/tcr-l.html

United Nations Crime and Justice Information Network

To subscribe visit http://www.topica.com/lists/uncjin-l@lserv.un.or.at and click on "Subscribe here." (This list had closed to the public by the time this book went to press.)

Criminology and Criminal Justice Announcement Lists

Some mailing lists simply send you information. They do not permit discussion among list members. They are called announcement lists. A number of criminal justice announcement lists provide very useful information. Primary among them are the following.

Cybercrime (dealing with all aspects of computer-related crime)
To subscribe send a blank e-mail message to:
cybercrime-subscribe@topica.com

Farislaw Bulletin (includes international and U. S. Supreme Court decisions) http://www.farislaw.com/lists.html
You can subscribe at the FARISLAW home page, or you can send e-mail to:

faris3-request@farislaw.com (for the HTML version) or
faris5-request@farislaw.com (for the text version)
Include the word SUBSCRIBE in the body of your message.

JUSTINFO (the newsletter of the National Criminal Justice Reference Service)
To subscribe send e-mail to listproc@aspensys.com
In the body of the message type: subscribe JUSTINFO *yourfirstname yourlastname* or visit NCJRS at http://www.ncjrs.org and click on "Subscribe to JUSTINFO." Then complete the form that appears on your screen.

The Juvenile Justice Newsletter
To subscribe send e-mail to: listproc@aspensys.com
In the body of the message type: subscribe JUVJUST *yourfirstname*
yourlastname

Legal Information Institute E-Mail Bulletins
http://www.law.cornell.edu/focus/bulletins.html
A service of the Cornell Law School.

The NCJRS Mailing List (keep up-to-date on federal crime and justice publications)
To subscribe visit NCJRS at http://www.ncjrs.org and click on "Join the NCJRS mailing list." Fill in the form that appears on your screen.

U. S. Supreme Court Opinions from the Legal Information Institute
To subscribe send e-mail to listserv@lii.law.cornell.edu
In the body of the message type: subscribe LIIBULLETIN *yourfirstname*
yourlastname

Discussion List Resources

A number of online resources can help you better understand how e-mail discussion lists work. Some sites are dedicated to helping you find the addresses of discussion groups that might be of interest to you. Still others provide listserver and discussion list catalogs and indexes, and a number provide the computer hardware and software that supports hundreds and even thousands of discussion groups. A list of such resources follows.

Catalog.com   http://catalog.com/vivian/interest-group-search.html

A list of lists.

Cyber Teddy   http://www.webcom.com/teddy/listserv.html

An online guide to mailing list information and newsgroups.

E-Mail Discussion Groups
http://www.nova.edu/Inter-Links/listserv.html

A service of Nova University.

IFLA's Internet Mailing Lists Guides and Resources
http://www.nlc-bnc.ca/ifla/I/training/listserv/lists.htm

A discussion of mailing lists and links to related resources.

Informundi
http://ourworld.compuserve.com/homepages/ajra/mailingl.htm

A PowerPoint presentation for a quick course on mailing lists. Try it. It's worthwhile!

The L-Soft List   http://www.lsoft.com/lists/listref.html
The catalog of LISTSERV lists!

List Bot   http://www.listbot.com
Run by MicroSoft, List Bot supports thousands of discussion groups, many of them in the area of crime and justice.

Liszt   http://www.liszt.com
Great for locating e-mail discussion lists and newsgroups. You can search by keyword. Over 50,000 topics are indexed here.

Neosoft.com   http://www.NeoSoft.com/internet/paml
Publicly accessible mailing lists.

Reference.com   http://www.reference.com
A mailing list and newsgroup directory.

Tile Net   http://www.tile.net/tile/listserv
A reference source for Internet discussion groups.

Topica   http://www.topica.com
Thousands of newsletters and discussion groups are available at Topica.

Yahoo! Groups   http://groups.yahoo.com
Supports one of the largest collections of discussion groups on the Internet today.

NEWSGROUPS

Some people compare **newsgroups** to virtual coffee shops, where friends gather to discuss topics of mutual interest. Like e-mail discussion lists, newsgroups are electronic forums. A newsgroup differs from an e-mail discussion list, however, in that messages contributed to the group remain on the server, available for review by anyone—including those new to the group. Newsgroups cover an enormous array of subjects and provide a way to quickly meet and connect with people from all over the world who share your interests.

> **Newsgroups:** electronic discussion forums consisting of collections of related postings (also called *articles*) on a particular topic that are posted to a news server, which then distributes them to other participating servers.[18]

Because our current system of Internet-based newsgroups grew out of a network called Usenet, newsgroups are often referred to as **Usenet newsgroups.** Newsgroups of today still reflect the original USENET framework.

It is not necessary to join a newsgroup in the same way that you join an e-mail discussion list. It is necessary, however, to have special newsreader software. Newsreader software comes bundled with most popular browser software, such as Netscape's Communicator and Microsoft's Internet Explorer. You can, if you wish, buy stand-alone newsreaders or download them from the Net.

Although newsgroups come and go, around 20,000 newsgroups exist on the Internet at any one time. The first time you log on to the Internet and start your newsreader software it will poll the news server operated by your Internet service provider in order to find out what newsgroups your ISP supports. Not every ISP supports all newsgroups, and it may be necessary to contact your ISP if you want to join an unsupported newsgroup.

Newsreader software requires you to choose which newsgroups you wish to subscribe to before it will display the messages those newsgroups contain. Subscribing consists merely of downloading a list of group-specific messages from your ISP's news server to your newsreader. Once you subscribe to a newsgroup and read some of the messages it contains, your newsreader software will remember what you've read. The next time you start up your newsreader it will check the groups to which you are subscribed and download the new messages that have been contributed since your last visit. If you join a lot of newsgroups, be prepared to wait a long time for the messages to be downloaded to your computer.

Before you subscribe to any newsgroup, however, it is a good idea to look for suitable groups by asking your newsreader software to search through all available newsgroups using search terms keyed to your interests. You might, for example, search for groups containing the words *crime* or *justice* in their titles. A search (in the spring of 2001) for newsgroups containing the word *crime* revealed the existence of the following newsgroups (not all of which were active at the time):

    alt.artcrime
    alt.crime
    alt.crime.bail-enforce
    alt.crime.peacemaking.criminology

alt.sex.net-abuse.hipcrime
alt.true-crime
alt.tv.crime-drama
asu.general.crime_stop
clari.local.california.sfbay.crime
clari.news.crime
clari.news.crime.abductions
clari.news.crime.assaults
clari.news.crime.fraud+embezzle
clari.news.crime.general
clari.news.crime.hate
clari.news.crime.issue
clari.news.crime.juvenile
clari.news.crime.misc
clari.news.crime.murders
clari.news.crime.murders.misc
clari.news.crime.murders.political
clari.news.crime.organized
clari.news.crime.sex
clari.news.crime.theft
clari.news.crime.top
clari.news.crime.war
clari.web.news.crime.abductions

You might also want to review the two-part article "List of Active Newsgroups," available at one of the following newsgroups:

news.lists
news.groups
news.answers

You do not have to actively participate in a newsgroup discussion to read newsgroup messages. The messages are there for all to read—like pages in a book. If you want to contribute your own message, you can. Otherwise, as with e-mail discussion lists, you can be a lurker rather than a contributor.

'ZINES AND E-JOURNALS

A number of electronic journals (called **e-journals**) and electronic magazines (called **'zines**) are available on the Internet. An abbreviated list of the most interesting e-journals and 'zines in the law, criminology, and criminal justice areas follows.

Alabama Law Review   http://www.law.ua.edu/lawreview

Provides full-text reproductions of its articles on the Internet.

American Journal of Criminal Justice
http://www.criminology.fsu.edu/ajcj.html

The official journal of the Southen Criminal Justice Association. Only submission procedures are available online.

American University Law Review
http://www.wcl.american.edu/pub/journals/lawrev/aulrhome.htm

The oldest and the largest journal at the American University Washington College of Law. The range of articles *The Law Review* publishes is not limited to one particular area of law. Full text of some articles is available.

American University International Law Review
http://www.wcl.american.edu/pub/ilr/home.htm

An international law journal produced by law students at American University.

Cardozo Law Review
http://www.cardozo.yu.edu/cardlrev/index.html

An online version of the Cardozo Law Review, a student-edited publication of the Benjamin N. Cardozo School of Law at Yeshiva University. Full-text articles are provided.

Cornell Law Review   http://www.law.cornell.edu/clr

Florida State University Law Review
http://www.law.fsu.edu/journals/lawreview/index.html

Published by the FSU College of Law, the journal provides Adobe PDF versions of its articles online.

Indiana Law Journal   http://www.law.indiana.edu/ilj/ilj.html

Published quarterly by students of the Indiana University School of Law-Bloomington. Full-text articles of selected volumes are available online.

Indiana Journal of Global Legal Studies
http://www.law.indiana.edu/glsj/glsj.html

International Journal of Drug Testing
http://big.stpt.usf.edu/journal

Journal of Online Law
http://warthog.cc.wm.edu/law/publications/jol

Law Journal Extra   http://www.ljx.com

Mercer Law Review   http://review.law.mercer.edu/issueindex.cfm
Published by students at the Walter F. George School of Law of Mercer University (Georgia). The full text of articles from recent issues is available online.

Murdoch University Electronic Journal of Law
http://www.murdoch.edu.au/elaw

An Australian law journal available entirely online.

National Law Journal   http://www.ljextra.com/nlj

New England Law Review
http://www.nesl.edu/lawrev/lawrev.htm

Published on the Web by the New England School of Law.

Stanford Law & Policy Review
http://www.stanford.edu/group/SLPR

An academic journal concentrating on issues of law and public policy, published twice a year by the law students of Stanford Law School.

Stanford Journal of International Law
http://www-leland.stanford.edu/group/SJIL

Theoretical Criminology
http://www.sagepub.co.uk/frame.html?http://www.sagepub.co.uk/journals/details/j0064.html

An online interdisciplinary and international journal for the advancement of the theoretical aspects of criminology. Nonsubscribers may view sample articles and the tables of contents for past issues.

University of Colorado Law Review
http://stripe.Colorado.EDU/cololrev/Home.html

Villanova Law Review
http://vls.law.vill.edu/students/orgs/law-review

Washington and Lee Law Review
http://www.wlu.edu/~lawrev

Published quarterly by students of the Washington and Lee University School of Law. Full-text articles are available online.

Washburn Law Journal   http://washburnlaw.edu/wlj

Web Journal of Current Legal Issues   http://webjcli.ncl.ac.uk

A bimonthly electronic journal published by Blackstone Press, Ltd., in the United Kingdom, focusing on current legal issues, including judicial decisions, law reform, legislation, legal research, policy-related socio-legal research, legal information, and information technology and practice.

Western Criminology Review   http://wcr.sonoma.edu

The official journal of the Western Society of Criminology. Complete full-text articles in the field of criminology.

As you can see from this list, most of today's justice-related online journals are in the area of law. You can perform a full-text search of all law journals on the Internet and of law journal abstracts via the University Law Review Project at http://www.lawreview.org. Another resource is provided by All Law (http://www.alllaw.com/journals_and_periodicals/legal) and provides a general listing of law and justice journals which are at least partially available online. Visit the Coalition of Online Law Journals at http://www.urich.edu/~jolt/e-journals for information about additional online availability, and remember to check the *Talk Justice* Web site for URLs that may have changed.

USING THE WEB

Join at least one of the e-mail discussion lists described in this chapter, and subscribe to at least one of the newsgroups. Then do the following:

1. Read the messages being posted to both the discussion list and the newsgroup. What topics are being discussed? Are the discussions focused? Could they be better focused? How?

2. If you were to begin your own discussion list or newsgroup, what would it be about? What rules might you set for discussants to be sure that they stick to the theme of the list/group? How would you enforce those rules?

6

Search Engines
and Web Maps

I have found that a great part of the information I have was acquired by looking for something and finding something else on the way.

—*Franklin P. Adams*

Men don't stop to ask for directions on the
Information Superhighway either!

—*Anonymous*

CHAPTER OUTLINE

INTRODUCTION

The Web is a huge place (see Figure 6-1). The Internet information company Cyveillance estimates that nearly five billion Web pages resided on servers all over the world in mid-2001, and that approximately seven million more are being added every day![19] The sheer amount of information available can make it extremely difficult to find what you're looking for. Imagine the Library of Congress after an earthquake, when all the books have fallen off the shelves and the power has gone out. What chance would you have of finding a particular book if you were rummaging around through the tumbled books at night? Even a flash-light wouldn't help much. In fact, under such circumstances, you could spend a lifetime searching through all of the books in the library, and you still might not find what you're looking for!

Fortunately for Web surfers, a number of search services, sometimes called *search engines*, have already done the job of categorizing most of the Web's content—and they continue to index new pages almost as fast as they are added. Better yet, almost all of these services are free! But, like anything else, it helps if you know how to use them.

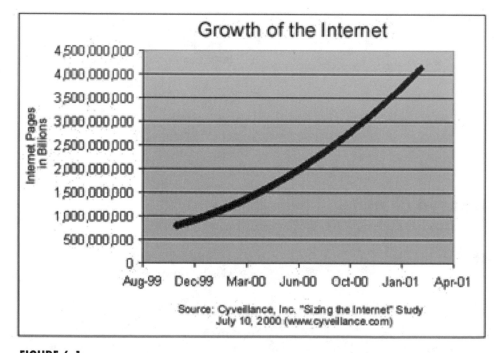

FIGURE 6-1
The growth of the Internet: August 1999-April 2001 (includes projections).
Source: Cyveillance, Inc. "Sizing the Internet" Study, July 10, 2000. (www.cyveillance.com/us/newsroom/pressr/000710/asp)

Search engines index Web pages using a number of strategies. Some, called *spiders* or *crawlers*, literally crawl across the Web and poll every site they find in order to determine that site's content. Others depend on human input (either from Web site designers, a staff of Web searchers, or both) to create directories of Web sites.

Technically speaking (although we don't want to get *too* technical), there are two main types of search facilities available on the web: **search engines** and **directories**. True search engines create their listings automatically, by crawling through the Web and indexing what they find. Directories depend on human input for the data they contain. Some search sites, of course, are hybridized—that is, they use both strategies in developing their content. For our purposes we will not distinguish between true search engines and directories, although you should be aware that the difference exists.

This chapter contains a list of most major search sites, broken down into simple search sites and metasearchers (search sites that poll more than one search engine). Some search engines—which we do not list here—are highly specialized. An excellent government-sponsored search tool called FirstGov (http://www.firstgov.gov or http://www.firstgov.com), for example, allows users to search the multitude of federal government sites populating the Web. Before you can use a search engine, however, it is best that you know some rules about how they work.

> **Search engine:** site-specific software and hardware that create indexes of Internet sites based on the titles of files, keywords, or the full text of files. Also, a tool for searching for information on the Internet by topic.

It is very important to remember that individual search engines have their own rules about how you should enter the information you are looking for. Most such engines are built around Boolean logic. **Boolean logic** was created by the English mathematician, George Boole, who developed a kind of algebra of logic. Boolean logic has become the basis for most computer database searches. It uses words called *operators* to determine whether a statement is true or false. Common Boolean operators are AND, OR, and NOT. Proper use of these three words can make your search far more fruitful than it might otherwise be. They can also save you an enormous amount of frustration when trying to find what you want.

If, for example, you want to learn more about crime rates in the United States, you might search for the term *crime* on the Web using a popular search engine. Doing so, however, will probably return thousands of hits. Another way to submit your search would be to type *crime* AND *rates* into the search field. Using the operator AND means that the search engine you are using will return the names and locations of documents containing both of the words *crime* and *rates*. If you were to type in *crime* OR *rates*, however, you would be inundated with a plethora of hits containing *either* the word *crime* or the word *rates*. You can also use the operator NOT as follows: *crime* NOT *England*. You will still receive many documents containing the word *crime*, but none that contain the word *England*. The NOT operator allows you to restrict your search.

Keep in mind that search sites differ, and that this general guide to using search engines may not apply to all sites. Some sites, for example, use the minus sign (–) instead of NOT, and some use the plus sign (+) in place of AND.

Many search sites allow you to search using a phrase. Some (but not all) require that you enclose the phrase in quotation marks. Hence, searching for the phrase "crime in the United States" might give you a better chance of finding the information you are looking for than looking for just *crime* AND *rates*. Of course, you might also want to search again using the phrase "crime in the U. S." since that is how the phrase might appear on a number of sites containing the data you seek.

Once the search site has returned a list of hits, you can click on the document that interests you the most. You can always use the "back" button on your browser to return to the results list provided by the search engine.

Some search facilities are topic-specific and limit searches to documents and information contained on that particular site. The interfaces used by such search facilities are generally far simpler than those that you will see when you visit major search engines. Even so, the principles that apply to site-specific searches are usually much the same as those that apply to searches of the entire Web. The NCJRS document database search page is shown, by way of example, in Figure 6-2.

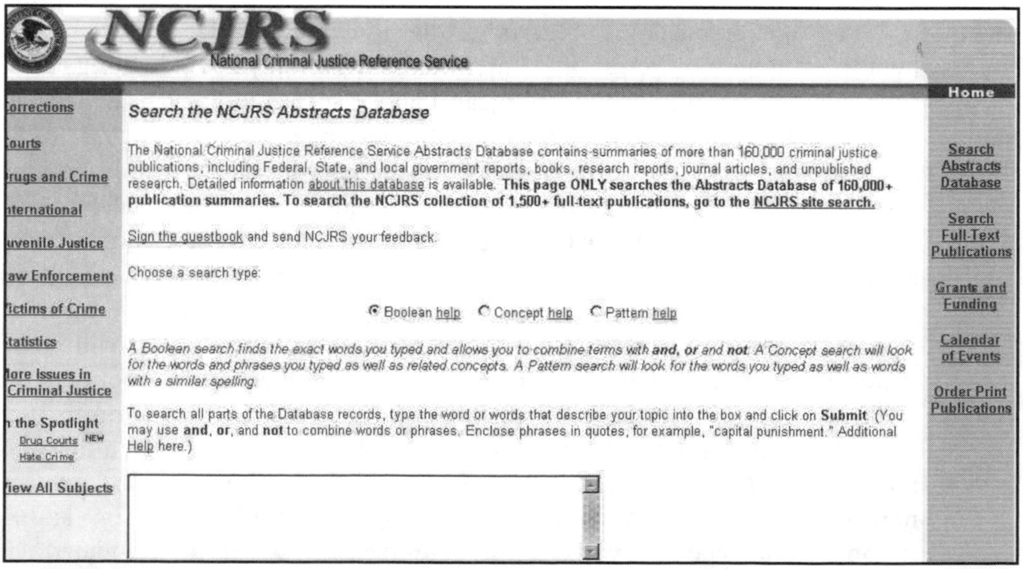

FIGURE 6-2
The NCJRS Abstracts database search page.

As mentioned previously, sites differ as to how they expect you to phrase your search. It is best to check with the search site to see what they require. Here, for example, is what the National Criminal Justice Reference Service has to say about conducting a search on the NCJRS Abstracts Database:[20]

HINTS ON SEARCHING

To search, simply type the word or words that describe your topic into the open search box and click on Submit. Enclose phrases in quotes. For example:

> gangs
> "drug court"

Choosing a Query Type: Concept, Pattern, and Boolean Searching

A **Boolean search** finds exactly the words you typed and allows you to combine terms with *and*, *or*, and *not* as well as parentheses ( ). For example, if you are searching for information on HIV/AIDS in correctional facilities you could enter:

> (AIDS or HIV) and (correctional or prison or jail)

A **Concept search** will look for the words and phrases you typed as well as related concepts. A **Pattern search** will look for the words you typed as well as words with a similar spelling; this is useful when you are not sure how to spell a word or a person's name.

Wildcard and Proximity Searching

To search on a word root with a variety of endings, use the *. For example, *correction** will find the words *correction*, *corrections*, or *correctional*. Also use the * to allow for plurals: for example, type *juvenile** to find the words *juvenile* or *juveniles*.

You can also search for words to be found within a specified number of words of each other. The pattern to follow is:

> word1 word2 within N

This means that word1 must be found within N words of word2. For example:

> mothers incarcerated within 10

will find the word *mothers* within 10 words of the word *incarcerated*.

If You Find Too Much

>> Instead of using the large search box for a global search, type your search terms in the Subject Search box.
>> Limit your search by date.
>> Make your wording more specific. Remember that all of the publications deal with criminal justice, so words like *crime* or *police* will bring back too much.
>> Choose a Boolean search instead of a Concept search. A Boolean search will find all of the terms you type in, while a Concept search may find documents which contain only some of the terms you typed, or may find words that are related but not exactly what you typed.

If You Find Too Little

>> Remove one of the terms from your search. If you are using too many terms connected with *and*, you may be restricting your search too much.

>> Change one of the terms to a broader term. For example, replace "*juvenile gangs*" with *gangs*.

>> Try to think of synonyms or related words and combine them with OR, selecting a Boolean search. For example:
>> "death penalty" or "capital punishment"
>> (police or "law enforcement") and California
>> (narcotics or drugs) and (adolescents or juveniles)

>> Allow for plurals with the * . For example, *prison** will find *prison* or *prisons* (as well as *prisoners*, etc.)

>> Look for misspellings in the terms you have entered.

GLOBAL SEARCH

Using the large search box will find the words you type anywhere in the record (except for some technical fields). This will search titles, short annotations, subject headings, authors, and NCJ numbers, as well as publishers, sponsoring agencies, journal citations, and abstracts.

SUBJECT SEARCH

This search is more focused than the global search, as it searches for the words you type only in each publication's title, in a one to two sentence description of the publication, and in the publication's subject headings (terms from the National Criminal Justice Thesaurus).

AUTHOR SEARCH

This search looks only for authors' and editors' names, including the names of people and organizations. When searching for a person's name, do not type in first names, as only first initials appear in the database. To search for articles by Jane Smith, type in

"j smith"

This will find the initial j adjacent to the word **smith**. Be sure to use quotation marks as shown to search for an exact phrase.

NCJ NUMBER SEARCH

All publications in the database have a six-digit number called an "NCJ" number or an "ACCN" (accession) number. For example, to search for NCJ 158544, type:

158544

LIMIT BY DATE

To limit by date, type start date and end date, for example:

To search for documents published in the years 1990 through 1998 Inclusive:
1/1/90-12/31/98
Spacing is important—do not leave any space around the dash.
To search for a specific year, for example, 1994:

1/1/94-12/31/94
Spacing is important—do not leave any space around the dash.

If you do not restrict your search by date, it will retrieve documents from the entire database, from the early 1970's on (with the most recent documents listed first).

Northern Light, on the other hand, one of the Web's newer search sites, uses a somewhat different set of search rules. Here's a few of the instructions you can find on the Northern Light help page on how to enter searches.[21]

OPTIMIZE YOUR SEARCH

To increase the precision of your search results, Northern Light requires most of the words in your search to be present in the result documents. To gain more control over your results, please read through the following hints.

>> Northern Light supports natural language searching. To find information on your topic of interest, try typing a question into the search bar. Example:

What is the capital of Sweden?

You can also search on simple words. The more words you enter, the more on-target your results will be. Examples:

ski resorts Vermont
(instead of **skiing**)

ergonomic workstation mouse keyboard
(instead of **ergonomics**)

>> Northern Light supports full Boolean capability (**AND, OR, NOT**), including parenthetical expressions, in all search forms. There is no limit to the level of nesting which you can use in a query.

If Boolean operators appear in quotes, or as part of a quoted phrase, they will be interpreted as a search term or part of a search term, rather than a Boolean operator. For example:

"War AND Peace"
will return documents with the phrase "War and Peace" (such as discussion of the book by Leo Tolstoy), whereas

War AND Peace
will return documents that contain the word War and the word Peace.

>> Use **OR** to retrieve documents that include *any* of the search words (rather than most). Example:

encryption OR cryptography

>> Use **NOT** to indicate a word that must *not* appear in the documents. Example:

dolphins NOT NFL

>> Use double quotes around specific phrases to focus your search on occurrences of the actual phrase. Examples:

recipes for "chocolate cake"
"General Dynamics"

Searches in single quotes will return the same results as returns that are not quoted.

>> In addition to **AND** and **NOT**, you may use a + (plus) to indicate words that **must** be present in the documents and a – (minus) for those that **must not** be present.

You must include a space between the + and – symbols and the terms which immediately precede them, but not between the symbols and the terms that follow them. Examples:

+dolphins –NFL
+recipes for + "chocolate cake" –nuts

>> Northern Light supports two truncation symbols (wildcards) in queries. You must have at least four non-wildcard characters in a word before you introduce a wildcard. The * (asterisk) can be used to replace multiple characters. The % (percent) symbol is used to replace only one character. Please note that Northern Light automatically stems most common plural and singular forms of words (a search on **cat** will also return results containing the word **cats**, and a search on **cats** will return results containing the word **cat**). Examples:

chemi* will find results containing words that begin with 'chemi' (e.g., chemical, chemistry, chemist)
psych*ist will find all results which contain words that begin and end with 'psych' and 'ist' (e.g., psychologist, psychiatrist)
gene%logy will return sites containing words beginning with 'gene' and ending with 'logy,' separated by a single letter (e.g., genealogy and geneology). *Useful for commonly misspelled words*

You can also use multiple truncation symbols within a single word. Expanded words found by using truncation symbols will not affect the relevancy ranking of those sites, so you may want to use additional related terms in your query to ensure that your results are accurate and meaningful.

A word of warning is in order about any information you get off of the Internet: It may not be reliable. Keep in mind that anyone can publish literally anything on the Net—and frequently they do. The reliability and authenticity of information posted on the Net is always in question. Unless the information is posted by a well-known source such as the Department of Justice or the National Criminal Justice Reference Service, it is best to either double-check the information before you use it or add a disclaimer to any material you produce that uses the information. If you are writing a term paper, for example, your instructor may ask that you use only sources on the Web known to be reliable and that you note the source of all information you gather from the Web. We don't have the space to discuss Internet citations in detail. Some manuals are starting to list the proper format for Web citations. Generally, however, Web materials may be cited as follows:

The Justice Research Association, "Rules for Posting." Web posted at http://talkjustice.com/rules.htm. Accessed April 2, 2001.

Finally, you should keep in mind that Web search tools differ in a number of other ways. Some search only top-level domains, meaning that they don't look at Web pages in subdirectories. Others index every word on every page they can find (regardless of level). Still others attempt to index images, video, and audio files as well as text. It is best to familiarize yourself with the various search sites that are available and to learn something about the kinds of results they can be expected to return, along with their rules for entering search terms, before you decide which is right for you.

HOW SEARCH ENGINES WORK

If you are interested in how search engines work you should visit Search Engine Watch and read the site's page titled "How Search Engines Work" (http://searchenginewatch.internet.com/webmasters/work.html). Search Engine Watch also provides statistics showing how some of the major search sites compare. A few statistics, drawn from the site, are shown in Figure 6-3. There are, of course, many different ways to compare search engines—and the number of sites each has indexed is just one way. You can visit Search Engine Showdown (http://www.searchengineshowdown.com) for a comprehensive survey of search engine sizes, along with estimates of dead links and other data. The site includes useful reviews of each of the major search engines.

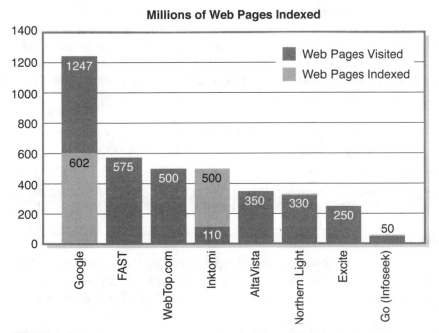

FIGURE 6-3

Web pages indexed by the major search engines as of November 1, 2000.

WEB SEARCH ENGINES

Search Engine Sites

About.com http://www.about.com

Uses a structured system of inclusive categories supported by expert guides in each area. An About search returns three sets of results: (1) matches from About's internal directory, (2) matches from the Web, and (3) matches from About partner sites.

Alta Vista http://www.altavista.digital.com

An advanced search engine with numerous capabilities. Alta Vista can be personalized, and has become a mainstay of many Web searchers. It's very powerful and flexible.

Ask Jeeves http://www.askjeeves.com

Allows you to enter plain language searches. Use full sentences if you want. Results tend to be less comprehensive than searches based on Boolean terminology.

Excite! http://www.excite.com

A mainstream search engine. If you are using Windows 95, Windows 98, or Windows NT, Excite! provides free software for integration into your browser. The software, called Excite! Direct, adds an Excite! logo to your browser toolbar and allows you to search Excite! quickly and conveniently without having to visit excite.com first. You can download the free software by visiting http://www.excite.com/direct.

Fast Search http://www.alltheweb.com

Claims to have indexed 575 million URLs. Users at the Justice Research Association found Fast Search produced the largest number of hits of any of the search engines listed here—including metasearchers. You can customize Fast Search or download a search tool that links to the site from your desktop.

Go http://www.go.com

Formerly known as InfoSeek, this site provides a kind of informational newspaper showcasing current topics of interest, including horoscopes, games, quotations, recipes, restaurants, movies, TV, weather forecasts, and famous people.

GoTo http://www.goto.com

GoTo got its start in late 1997, and was developed in response to the need for a new kind of search engine that would be simple, fast, and relevant. GoTo lives by the phrase "Search made simple." Sites that pay for listings tend to show up higher in the results.

Google   http://www.google.com

Google organizes the Web by topic. When performing a complex search, Google ranks pages by relevance and shows the most relevant pages first. *PC Magazine* (December 5, 2000) ranks Google the best search engine for general use.

HotBot   http://www.hotbot.com

A very capable search engine that provides users with many options for fine tuning a search. One of the best engines for highly targeted and refined searches.

I Find   http://www.inference.com/ifind

An "intelligent massively fast parallel" Web searcher.

IWon   http://www.iwon.com

Organized around a vast array of informational categories, and backed by CBS TV, IWon gives you points for each search you conduct. Points qualify you for cash prizes awarded in daily, weekly, monthly, and annual drawings.

Lycos   http://www.lycos.com

A venerable and reliable search site. Lycos ranks sites according to relevance and popularity. In October 1998, Lycos purchased the competing HotBot search service, which continues to be run separately.

Magellan   http://magellan.excite.com

One of the first search sites on the Web.

Netfind   http://www.aol.com/netfind

A Net search service sponsored by America Online. You can easily reach the AOL search site via http://aol.com. AOL Search is especially useful for AOL members who can use it to search the Web as well as AOL-specific content.

Northern Light   http://www.nlsearch.com

A relatively new search service that uses "Custom Search Folders" and an integrated results list of Web and premium information. *PC Magazine* (December 5, 2000) ranks Northern Light on a par with Google.

Webcrawler   http://webcrawler.com

Webseek   http://www.ctr.columbia.edu/webseek

Yahoo!   http://www.yahoo.com

Perhaps the best-known search service on the Net. Provides text and file searches, people finder, chat, and more. Unlike many search services that spider the Web to build their indexes, Yahoo! is based on a human-compiled directory.

Zamboni's Searchers   http://www.iglou.com/zamboni/search.html

A collection of search engines. Choose which one you want to search.

METASEARCHING

Metasearchers, also known as multisearchers or parallel search engines, poll many search engines with whatever search term or phrase you enter. If you use these combination search services you are said to be "conducting a metasearch," or **metasearching**. Metasearchers are a lot like huge search engines in that they help compile results from many different sources. Metasearchers organize their results into a uniform format, which they then display to you.

> **Metasearcher:** a search engine that searches many different search sites simultaneously.

A list of most metasearchers is available via one Web page, Dr. Webster's Big Page of Search Engines, which can be reached at http://www.123go.com/drw/search/metasearch.htm. A second source for metasearchers is the Web Developer's Virtual Library at http://www.stars.com/Location/Meta/Searchers.html. A site that allows you to metasearch the metasearchers is MetaPleth by SpaceSearch Lite. You can reach MetaPleth at http://www.ee.surrey.ac.uk/Personal/L.Wood/spacesearch/metapleth.

Metasearcher Sites

Here's a list of metasearchers that you may find useful.

Cyber411 Parallel Search Engine
http://helios.unive.it/franz/cyber.html

Cyber411 sends your query to fifteen different search engines simultaneously.

Dogpile   http://www.dogpile.com

A respected metasearcher with an unusual name.

Highway 61   http://www.highway61.com

Submits your query to the six largest search engines simultaneously.

Inference Find   http://www.inference.com/ifind

A great metasearching tool that queries the major search engines, merges the results, removes redundancies, and gathers the hits into groups of links based on your request.

Mamma   http://www.mamma.com

A smart parallel search engine with much to recommend it.

MetaCrawler   http://www.metacrawler.com

MetaCrawler sends your queries to many different search engines, including Alta Vista, Excite!, InfoSeek, Lycos, WebCrawler, and Yahoo!.

MetaFind   http://search.metafind.com

Organizes results in an easy-to-use manner.

My Starting Point   http://www.stpt.com

Provides free e-mail along with e-mail newsletters featuring news and information about the site. Also offers a selection of "Best of the Web" sites and e-shopping.

Profusion   http://www.profusion.com

You can ask Profusion to search the "best three," or "fastest three" search engines, or tailor your search by selecting the search engines you want to poll.

Search.com   http://www.search.com

A service of CNet, one of the Web's most comprehensive content providers. Simultaneously searches Alta Vista, Direct Hit, FindWhat, GoTo, Keen, mySimon, Sprinks, and Yahoo! for the terms or phrases you enter.

Search Onramp   http://search.onramp.net

Ranks and scores the results of a simultaneous search of many engines.

A number of proprietary software tools are available today that can perform metasearches with more options than are generally available in Web-based metasearches. Copernic (http://www.copernic.com), for example, polls more than eighty different search engines and presents the results in collated fashion, allowing you to download results pages. In order to use Copernic, you must download a small free program that resides on your computer. The program removes duplicates and dead links, and permits you to search within results. You can register the program and upgrade to Copernic 2000 Plus, which will search 610 engines.

Blue Squirrel's WebSeeker® (http://www.bluesquirrel.com/products/seeker/webseeker.html), which polls over 100 search engines to find the results you want, also turns your computer into a personal metasearcher. Like Copernic, it gives you the ability to browse the results returned by your search, even allowing you to save metasearch results on your computer as HTML files for later use. WebSeeker can be set to routinely go out and automatically search and update your disk-based index, working transparently in the background while you use your computer for other things. Similar products are available in BullsEye (http://www.intelliseek.com) and WebFerret (http://www.ferretsoft.com/netferret). BullsEye, from Intelliseek, is described by its manufacturer as an "Intelligent Desktop Portal." The latest version promises instant access to relevant, targeted, and personalized information through the use of over 800 search engines and databases. BullsEye offers news searches from hundreds of news wires, comparison shopping, and quick report generating.

Many of the major search engines also make it possible for you to download and install specialized browser toolbars that link directly to the service that provides them. If you download the Google bar, for example, the next time you run Internet Explorer you will see a Google search box in your browser bar. Type a word or phrase into the search box, hit the return key, and Google will display the search results in your browser window. Browser toolbars like Google's make it unnecessary to visit the search engine site in order to begin your search.

However, it is not necessary to purchase software or to install specialized browser bars on your computer to conduct effective searches. Most likely, a simple but effective way to search the Web already exists right on your desktop. That's because many of today's major browsers have a search feature built in. The feature is usually displayed right on the browser's toolbar. Both Explorer and Communicator label the feature plainly enough, calling it "search." Although such built-in search features do not necessarily have the full functionality of metasearchers, and they may not allow you to choose the specific search engine you want to use (they often provide a limited selection of engines from which you can select a default), they do provide you with easy access to a simple search function. Click the "search" button on your browser and you will see what we mean!

Learn more about Web searching and search engines and tools at Search Engine Watch (http://www.searchenginewatch.com). Search Engine Watch offers reviews of all majors search engines, search tips, information on search strategies, and more. The site lists a multitude of specialized search engines that you won't find anywhere else, and a free search engine newsletter is available via e-mail.

USING THE WEB

Visit three of the search sites and three of the metasearch engines listed in this chapter. At each site, search for a topic of special interest, such as "international criminal justice," "community policing," or the "classical school of criminology." Then answer these questions:

1. What did you learn about phrasing your searches? Is it best to search for a single word, to combine words with AND, or to use a search phrase?

2. If you want to use a phrase, how does each site require you to enter it? What are the differences between each of the sites in this regard?

3. Did you find that metasearch engines worked better than stand-alone search sites? On what do you base your answer?

7

Netiquette and Web Manners

Technology is driving the future; the steering is up to us.

—*Computer Professionals for Social Responsibility[22]*

When thou enter a city, abide by its customs.

—*The Talmud*

CHAPTER OUTLINE

INTRODUCTION

The early days of the personal computer brought with them efforts by a number of concerned groups to educate computer owners in how to use their machines ethically and with a sense of social responsibility. The Computer Ethics Institute,[23] for example, issued its "Ten Commandments for Computer Ethics" a number of years ago. The commandments[24] are reproduced in Figure 7-1.

The advent of the Internet has made ethical issues associated with the use of computers far more important today than they were in the early days of personal computing. That is because the Net is largely an ungoverned entity—making the need for self-control and an awareness of social responsibility a crucial issue among Net surfers. Today's Net citizens and Web site builders have a great deal of freedom as to what they can post on the Web, what kinds of e-mail messages they can send, what kind of Web sites they build, and the content they choose to contribute to newsgroups.

Today's ethical questions take many forms: (1) What's the purpose of the Internet and the Web? What should they be used for? (2) Should there be limits on how they are used? Should anybody be able to use the Net for anything they choose—so long as it is not blatantly criminal in purpose? (3) What is proper conduct for individual members of the online community? (4) How can informal standards be established and communicated? (5) How can they be enforced?

---

1. Thou shalt not use a computer to harm other people.
2. Thou shalt not interfere with other people's computer work.
3. Thou shalt not snoop around in other people's files.
4. Thou shalt not use a computer to steal.
5. Thou shalt not use a computer to bear false witness.
6. Thou shalt not use or copy software for which you have not paid.
7. Thou shalt not use other people's computer resources without authorization.
8. Thou shalt not appropriate other people's intellectual output.
9. Thou shalt think about the social consequences of the program you write.
10. Thou shalt use a computer in ways that show consideration and respect.

FIGURE 7-1
The Ten Commandments of Computer Ethics.
Source: Computer Ethics Institute. Web posted at http://www.cpsr.org/program/ethics/cei.html. Reprinted with permission. Copyright © 1991 Computer Ethics Institute.

Should they be? (6) How much influence should the government have over Web content and personal online communications?

A serious ethical problem facing today's Net citizens, for example, is the huge amount of junk e-mail making its way into e-mail boxes everywhere. It is not unusual for anyone with an e-mail address to constantly receive numerous e-mail messages advertising get-rich schemes and a huge array of products that almost no one wants. Junk e-mail is not necessarily against the law, although the U. S. Congress is considering legislation intended to curb e-mail abuse. Some of the legislation now being considered requires that senders of unsolicited e-mail include contact information along with instructions on how to be removed from the e-mail list from which the unsolicited mail originated. Some people receive hundreds of junk e-mail messages a day as a result of their e-mail address being on a mass-mailing list used by **spammers**. Spammers are people who sell mailing lists to one another, and if you end up on one spammer's list, you can be sure that you will soon be on many others. If that happens, the amount of junk e-mail you receive can grow to astronomical proportions—causing legitimate e-mail to get lost in the flood of messages received.

> **Spammers:** unscrupulous individuals and companies who clutter the Net with unsolicited junk e-mail.

To address the problem, most e-mail software allows you to set filters, rejecting messages with certain keywords or key phrases in their subject lines (e.g., "get rich quick") or mail coming from certain addresses. Of course, spammers are smart enough to regularly change their e-mail addresses and to use a wide variety of catchy phrases in the subject lines of their messages, making it difficult to filter out all unwanted mail. If you are unable to end or significantly reduce the amount of **spam** you receive, you may find it necessary to change e-mail accounts. If you set too many filters in your e-mail program, you may successfully limit spam—but may end up filtering out much legitimate mail as well!

> **Spam:** junk e-mail indiscriminately sent to a lot of people. The process of sending such messages is called *spamming*.

If you are especially concerned about spam, or if you want to learn more about current legislation being considered to regulate unsolicited commercial e-mail, you might want to visit the Coalition Against Unsolicited Commercial E-mail (CAUCE). CAUCE is an all-volunteer organization formed to advocate legislative solutions to the spam problem. You can visit CAUCE on the Web at http://www.cauce.org. The Federal Trade Commission (FTC) offers resources for fighting spam through Project Mailbox, a site intended to help consumers, businesses, and law enforcement agencies deal with scam artists who use electronic mail to perpetrate fraud. The site uses the rather catchy phrase "Catch

the Bandit in Your Mailbox." You can reach it at http://www.ftc.gov/bcp/
conline/edcams/mailbox/index.html. If you think you've been victimized, you
can even file a complaint with the FTC online.

Other than spam, many potential ethical and interpersonal problems per-
meate the Net. Sex sites, offering total nudity, live sex acts via computer, and
deviant sexual antics, abound. Some people say that there are more sex sites on the
Web than any other category of site, and such sites are reputed to be the biggest
moneymakers on the Web. Whether or not triple-X content should be available on
the Web and whether it should be available to all those (even children) who surf
the Web is an important issue that is receiving much attention today. The
Communications Decency Act, passed by Congress in 1996 in an effort to control
such sites, was largely overturned by the U. S. Supreme Court in 1997. Other
efforts are now under way in Congress to establish a rating system for all Web sites.
Sites would be required to display their assigned ratings prominently on their
home pages. Browsers could then read a site's rating and could be set by concerned
parents, employers, and others to prevent access to certain types of sites.

Another area—that of interpersonal communications—provides an especially difficult challenge from an ethical standpoint. Some people misrepresent
themselves during e-mail communications. They may claim, for example, to be
female when they are actually male (and vice versa). Others may claim to be looking for love even though they are married. A few people offer sexual services for
sale, and still others attempt to gain sympathy in order to receive money and
donations. Some send bogus e-mail designed to have recipients relinquish their
charge-card numbers or bank account information. They then sell this information to criminals who use the acquired charge-card numbers to make fraudulent
purchases. Quite a few unethical Net citizens run scams, selling nonexistent products in bogus schemes to get money. Just about any kind of illegal scam you can
think of that has been perpetrated among people in the physical world can be
found in cyberspace today.

By far the most common problem on the Net today is the relatively unin-
hibited flow of hostile and/or obscene interpersonal communications. People in
discussion groups are especially likely to receive abusive messages when they post
opinions that may be unpopular with others. E-mail messages that berate other
people, often with obscene terminology, are called **flames**, and the process of sending such messages is called **flaming**.

> **Flames:** abusive, obscene, and distasteful messages generally directed at
> a particular individual. The sending of such messages is called *flaming*.

Anyone interested in exploring computer ethics in more detail can visit the
Center for Applied Ethics page on Computer and Information Ethics Resources on

the World Wide Web at http://www.ethics.ubc.ca/resources/computer/topics.html. The site contains online codes of ethics, advice for keeping children safe on the Web, copyright codes, digital communications initiatives, links to ethics in technology sites, and much more.

WHAT IS NETIQUETTE?

Not all of the Net's problems can be solved overnight. Nonetheless, there is much that you, as an individual, can do *now* to improve the Net. By following a few simple rules of **netiquette**, you can make the Net a much better place for yourself and others. The term *netiquette* refers to a set of rules for behaving properly online, and most netiquette is concerned with online communications. Figure 7-2 displays what Virginia Shea, a prolific writer in the area of netiquette, calls the "core rules of netiquette."

> **Netiquette:** network etiquette, the do's and don'ts of online communication.[25] Also, the etiquette of cyberspace.

Shea says that all 10 rules essentially boil down to one: *Remember the human.* By that she means that we must always remember that when we are online we are not interacting merely with impersonal computers or with an impersonal network. At the other end of our e-mail messages or discussion group contributions, says Shea, there are always other human beings. We cannot treat those human beings as though they are machines without feelings. In other words, if we are to be ethical actors in cyberspace, we cannot confuse the impersonal medium of the Internet with the people who populate it.

Remember the human is a good rule. It is easy to be offensive online, however, without meaning to be. That is because cyberspace, like anyplace else with a unique culture, has its own set of rules and standards. Violate them and you will be considered rude or offensive.

What follows is a short summary of netiquette guidelines. This summary has been adapted from RFC 1855, a working document which originated with Intel Corporation employees seeking to stimulate thought about ethical behavior on the Net. The guidelines printed here deal with three areas of Net use: (1) e-mail communications, (2) mailing lists and newsgroups, and (3) other interactive services such as Internet Relay Chat. You can find the full text of RFC 1855 at http://www.april.org/association/netiquette.html and at http://www.cybernothing.org/cno/docs/rfc1855.html. The recommendations that follow are not rules, but are meant only to advise you on how to conduct yourself on the Net.

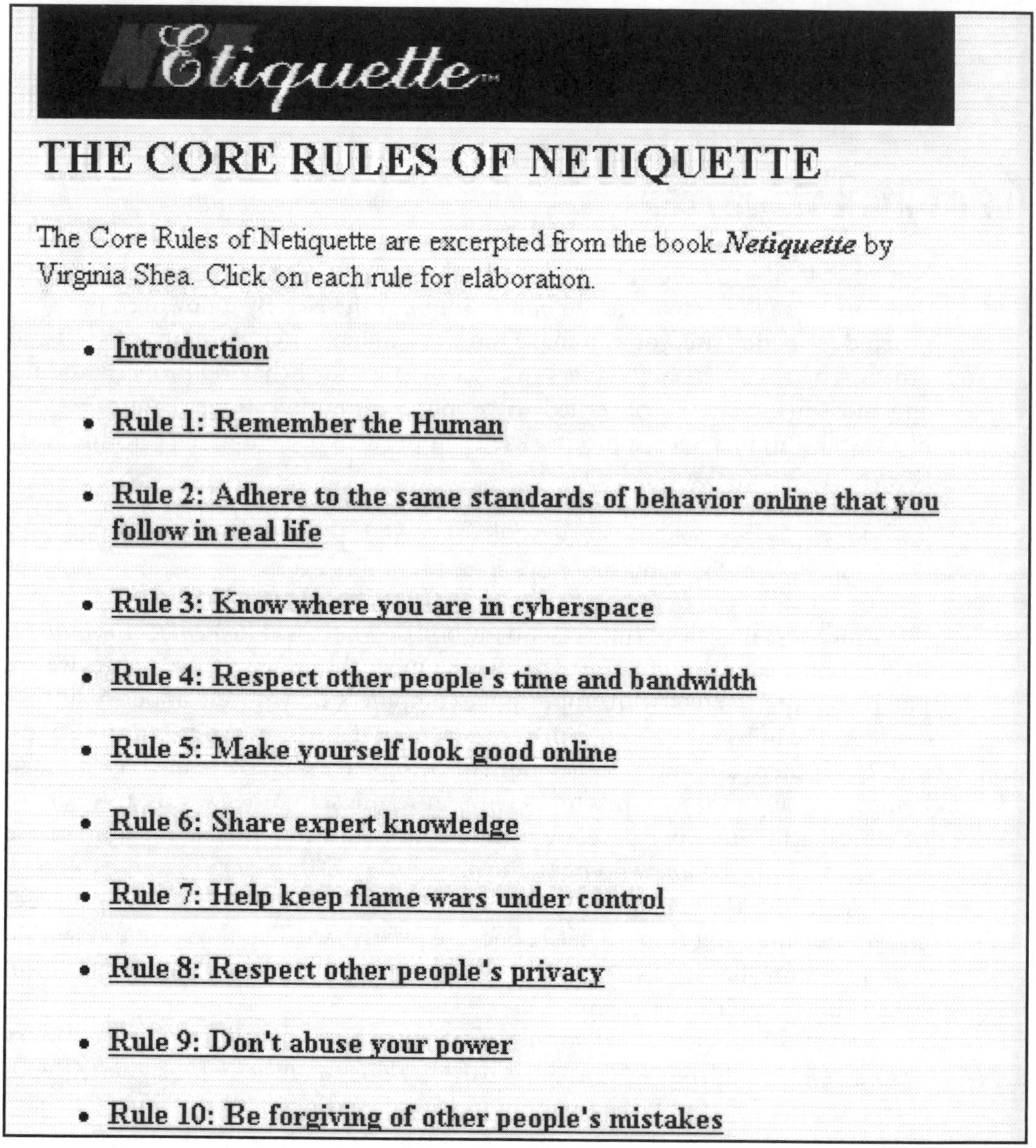

Etiquette™

THE CORE RULES OF NETIQUETTE

The Core Rules of Netiquette are excerpted from the book *Netiquette* by Virginia Shea. Click on each rule for elaboration.

- Introduction

- Rule 1: Remember the Human

- Rule 2: Adhere to the same standards of behavior online that you follow in real life

- Rule 3: Know where you are in cyberspace

- Rule 4: Respect other people's time and bandwidth

- Rule 5: Make yourself look good online

- Rule 6: Share expert knowledge

- Rule 7: Help keep flame wars under control

- Rule 8: Respect other people's privacy

- Rule 9: Don't abuse your power

- Rule 10: Be forgiving of other people's mistakes

FIGURE 7-2
The core rules of Netiquette. Web posted at http://www.albion.com/netiquette/corerules.html.
Screenshot courtesy of Albion.com.

E-Mail

>> If your Internet access is through a corporate account, check with your employer about his or her policy regarding private e-mail.

>> Don't assume any Internet communication is completely secure. Never include in an e-mail message anything you would not put on a postcard.

>> Independently verify any suspect mail you receive—especially if it contains important content—as e-mail return addresses can easily be forged.

>> If you are forwarding or reposting a message, don't change the original wording.

>> Remember that it is considered very impolite to forward someone's e-mail message to another person without the author's permission.

>> When responding to a previous post, include the relevant parts of the original message. That way it will be clear what you are responding to.

>> If you are replying to a message, quote only the relevant parts—not the entire message (especially if it is a very lengthy message you are responding to).

>> Do not send chain letters, especially those involving moneymaking pyramid schemes. They are highly frowned upon by Internet culture and can make you look like a fool.

>> Do not send abusive or heated messages (flames) or obscenity over the Internet.

>> Don't send flame bait. That is, don't send messages that are sure to offend people you are communicating with.

>> If you receive a flame, it is best to ignore it.

>> Be careful about using sarcasm or irony. Readers can't see your facial expressions or hear your tone of voice. Statements that you intend as jokes can be taken seriously.

>> Remember that no one can hear your tone of voice. Use **emoticons** to express what you are feeling. Signal jokes by using a smiley such as :-). However, do *not* overuse emoticons.

>> Use only e-mail abbreviations that you are sure of, or you may have readers ROTFL (rolling on the floor laughing).

>> Take care with addressing mail. Carefully read the "To:" and "Cc:" lines in your message before you send it. You can easily send mail to unintended recipients if you are not careful. *That* can be embarrassing.

>> Allow time for mail to be received and replied to before sending a follow-up message. Keep in mind that mail messages do not necessarily move as

fast as spoken words on the telephone and that people's work schedules and time differences around the world can result in delays.

>> Don't make your mail too long, unless the recipient is expecting a verbose message or unless a long message is truly necessary given the subject matter. Under normal circumstances an e-mail message longer than 100 lines of text is too long.

>> If you use a signature file, keep it short. Four to six lines is usually enough. Elaborate signatures with multiple addresses, lengthy quotations, and/or ASCII artwork just take up space in your recipients' mailboxes.

>> Remember, the Internet is a global community, and other people's values and outlook on life may be different from your own. Be tolerant in what you say and in how you respond to what others say.

>> Be careful with slang or phrases that may offend or that may not be understood in another region or country.

>> Use mixed-case letters when you type. UPPERCASE LOOKS AS IF YOU ARE SHOUTING and is generally considered offensive.

>> Use asterisks (*) before and after a word to give it emphasis.

>> Always include a subject header in your mail messages in order to let recipients know what the message is about before they read it.

>> If you have more than one topic to write about, send separate messages.

>> Spelling mistakes are distracting. Most e-mail software programs today have built-in spell checkers. Use the one in your program before posting your message.

>> Proofread. Grammatical errors are equally annoying.

>> Remember that unsolicited e-mail, especially if it contains advertising, is generally unwelcome (and is lawfully forbidden in some countries).

>> Know how your mail program works. Some mail and news editors, for example, only *appear* to insert line breaks—but actually don't. Your message recipients might see every paragraph as one immense line that scrolls far off their screens. You can learn what your mail and news editors do by sending a message to yourself (or by posting it to the newsgroup alt.test) and then reading the message in a couple of newsreaders.

>> When attaching files to your e-mail messages, try to keep them reasonably sized. You should consider using a compression program (like PKZIP) to reduce the size of files before sending them.

Mailing Lists and Newsgroups

>> Remember that messages posted to mailing lists and newsgroups are read by a large number of people.

>> Before joining a newsgroup or mailing list, you may want to be a lurker. That is, you might read what others in the list or group are saying in order to get a feel for the nature of the group before jumping in.

>> If posting to newsgroups, be aware that many are archived, and the archives are available for a very long time. Don't say anything that might come back to haunt you years down the road. It is generally not possible to retrieve messages once they have been sent.

>> Be very careful about advertising. Most groups look highly askance at anyone who posts advertisements to their group.

>> Do not make statements that can be interpreted as official positions of your organization or offers to do business.

>> Read FAQs (Frequently Asked Questions), if they are available, before posting a question to the group.

>> Keep your messages concise, and make them relevant to the group and to the topics being discussed by the group.

>> Don't post messages to inappropriate newsgroups.

>> Don't get involved in or respond to flame wars.

>> If you find a newsgroup or a topic offensive, avoid it or leave the group.

>> Keep private messages private. Don't post them to the group; send them instead to the person's private e-mail address.

>> Don't betray confidences. It's all too easy to quote a personal message by mistake in a message to the entire group.

Internet Relay Chat [IRC]

Internet Relay Chat (IRC) allows participants to enter into live, real-time conversations with other Internet users. Participants generally join a **channel** or a **chat room** centered on a shared topic of interest. The *Talk Justice* site, for example, makes real-time chat available to anyone with an interest in criminal and social justice.

Netiquette surrounding participation in IRC demands that you behave appropriately:

>> Respect the standards of the group you are talking to. It is generally a good idea to listen to a channel before participating in order to get a feel for the ground rules. After only a few minutes of listening, you should have an idea of what is and is not acceptable.

>> Remember, the world is a big place full of very different people. If you find subject matter that offends you, then don't join that chat channel.

>> Leave a channel that becomes offensive to you after you joined. Sometimes the course of a discussion changes, new people enter a chat area, or the

purpose of the channel changes. All these can have an adverse effect on how comfortable you feel in the chat channel.

>> Understand that unacceptable behavior on your part may get you banned from a channel or from the chat area.

NETIQUETTE RESOURCES

Some interesting netiquette sites can be found at the following addresses.

Albion.com   http://www.albion.com/netiquette/index.html

Albion's highly recommended Netiquette Home Page contains the following information: (1) links to both summary and detailed information about netiquette; (2) netiquette basics; (3) an overview of network etiquette excerpted from the book *Netiquette* by Virginia Shea (Shea has been called "the Ms. Manners of the Internet"); (4) a netiquette quiz designed to test your etiquette knowledge (requires a Java-compatible browser); (5) a netiquette table of contents with links to a wealth of netiquette information; and (6) a netiquette catalog page where you can order Virginia Shea's Net classic *Netiquette*. Albion also supports the "Netiquette Mailing List." In order to join the list, send e-mail to netiquette-request@albion.com with the words "subscribe YourFirstName YourLastName" as the *subject* of the message.

Arlene H. Rinaldi's Netiquette Home Page
http://www.fau.edu/rinaldi/netiquette.html

Rinaldi is a professor at Florida Atlantic University.

Emily Post News   http://www.clari.net/brad/emily.html

Some well-considered ideas on how to behave on the Net.

Netiquette in Brief   http://www.wiu.edu/users/mfbhl/wiu/netiquette.htm

A summary of netiquette principles.

The Netiquette Quiz
http://www.albion.com/netiquette/netiquiz.html

If your browser supports Java, you can test your netiquette knowledge at this site.

USING THE WEB

In this chapter we were able to spend only a brief amount of time discussing netiquette. In order to gain a more complete knowledge of the subject, you should visit at least two of the netiquette resource sites described in this chapter. Then answer the following questions:

1. What significant areas of netiquette information were excluded from this chapter (but found at the sites)? Describe each area in some detail.

2. Do you disagree with any of the principles of netiquette listed on any of these sites? If so, why? With which do you most agree? Why?

3. Are there any forms of netiquette that you feel have not been addressed by this guide and the sites you visited? If so, what are they?

8

Criminal Justice Careers Online

Work is life, you know, and without it, there's nothing but fear and insecurity.

—John Lennon (1940-80), British rock musician[26]

Work expands so as to fill the time available for its completion.

—Parkinson's Law[27]

CHAPTER OUTLINE

FINDING EMPLOYMENT ONLINE

Not long ago, finding a job took a lot of legwork. Job seekers had to read newspapers, subscribe to special employment services, and sometimes travel considerable distances to investigate local job markets. While applying for a job today is still one of the most daunting experiences facing recent college graduates, the process has been made a lot easier by online job banks and electronic employment services.

Some sites, such as Government Jobs.Com (http://www.govtjobs.com), are designed to make your job search efficient. No fees are charged to search the site. Although the site is private, job openings are frequently posted by government agencies, including those at federal, state, and local levels. Job search firms and advertising agencies also advertise vacant positions on the service. Although employers must pay a fee to advertise, potential employees can search all job vacancies for free.[28]

Each Government Jobs.Com listing includes the position title, a description of the position, job requirements (education, special skills, etc.), duties/responsibilities, salary if given, closing date, name of agency, and any other information pertinent to the position. In addition to job listings, Government Jobs.Com provides job resource information by state, including job-line phone numbers, city and county leagues and associations, statewide newspapers, and so forth. It also includes links to municipal and county government Web sites.

The federal government maintains a number of job-listing services on the Web and uses such sites as recruitment tools. One of the most popular is FedWorld (you can reach the jobs page at http://www.fedworld.gov/jobs/jobsearch.html). If you visit FedWorld you can also click on a selection that reads "Sign up to get FedWorld Vacancy Announcements via Email." Fill out the form that appears, send it to the FedWorld server, and you will quickly find job announcements appearing in your e-mail box. FedWorld also makes available some shareware software packages containing federal job application forms OF612 and SF171, which many people use to apply for federal jobs.

Many individual criminal justice agencies also post job vacancies as well as entry requirements on the Web. The FBI special agent information page, for example, reads as follows:[29]

ENTRY REQUIREMENTS

To carry out its mission, the FBI needs men and women who can fill a variety of demanding positions. To qualify for training as an FBI Special Agent, you must be a U.S. citizen, or a citizen of the Northern Mariana Islands, at least 23 and not have reached your 37th birthday on appointment. Candidates must be completely available for assignment anywhere in the FBI's jurisdiction, have uncorrected vision not worse than 20/200 (Snellen) and corrected 20/20 in one eye and not worse than 20/40 in the other eye. All candidates must pass a color vision test.

Special Agent applicants also must meet hearing standards by audiometer test. No applicant will be considered who exceeds the following: a) average hearing loss of 25 decibels (ANSI) at 1000, 2000, and 3000 Hertz; b) single reading of 35 decibels at 1000, 2000, and 3000 Hertz; c) single reading of 35 decibels at 500 Hertz; and d) single reading of 45 decibels at 4000 Hertz.

Candidates must possess a valid driver's license, and be in excellent physical condition with no defects which would interfere in firearm use, raids, or defensive tactics.

Applicants must possess a four-year degree from a college or university accredited by one of the regional or national institutional associations recognized by the United States Secretary of Education.

There are four entry programs: Law, Accounting, Language, and Diversified.

>>   **Law:** To qualify under the Law Program, you must have a JD degree from a resident law school.

>>   **Accounting:** To qualify under the Accounting Program, you must have a BS degree with a major in accounting or a related discipline, and be eligible to take the CPA examination. Candidates who have not passed the CPA exam will also be required to pass the FBI's Accounting test.

>>   **Language:** To qualify under the Language Program, you must have a BS or BA degree in any discipline and be proficient in a language that meets the needs of the FBI. Candidates will be expected to pass a Language Proficiency Test.

>>   **Diversified:** To qualify under the Diversified Program, you must have a BS or BA degree in any discipline, plus three years of full-time work experience, or an advanced degree accompanied by two years of full-time work experience.

Some agencies are now posting job application forms directly on the Web. You can complete these forms online, click the "submit" button at the end of the form, and apply for a job without ever leaving your chair in front of your computer. Figure 8-1, for example, shows an online application form for employment as a U. S. Border Patrol agent. You can find the form at http://www.usajobs.opm.gov/BPA1.HTM.

Significantly, a number of criminal justice-specific sites offer a wide range of useful services. Notable among these is AdviseNet© (see Figure 8-2). AdviseNet (http://courses.smsu.edu/mkc096f) bills itself as "The Incredible online Criminal Justice Adviser." As its name implies, AdviseNet© is a site that offers advice as well as other services. Although its primary targets are students studying in or graduating from university-level criminal justice programs, it is a useful site for any college student—regardless of major or minor. AdviseNet© contains over 175 folders of information and 2,400 links to sites and documents, but is designed to be navigated with great speed.

The AdviseNet© Main Menu consists of three major categories: Getting Started, Studying Criminal Justice, and Life After Graduation. The "Getting Started" section offers students tips on how to get better grades, write better term papers, make a good impression in class, succeed in other aspects of university life, and other useful information.

In the category called "Studying Criminal Justice," you can find answers to such questions as whether a student needs to major or minor in criminal justice

Border Patrol Agent On-Line Application

Welcome. You have reached the U.S. Government's World Wide Web application processing system. We are now accepting applications for Border Patrol Agent positions with the United States Immigration and Naturalization Service.

The vacancies to be filled are General Schedule grades 5 and 7. You will be presented with a series of questions that must be answered. Some questions will require a simple Yes or No response, while others may require you to select from a list of options, or require you to type information using the keyboard.

Please enter your 3-digit extension number now. If you do not know the extension number, please enter 999.

We are interested in knowing how you heard about this recruitment announcement for Border Patrol Agent positions. Indicate only one of the following numbers which was your primary source of information.

Ad in area newspaper.   ○
INS employee.   ○
INS Human Resources or Personnel Office.   ○
Ad in military base newspaper.   ○
Ad in college newspaper.   ○
College Career Planning Office, College Job Fair, or Faculty Member.   ○
USAJOBS, Federal Job Opportunities Board, Federal Job Information Touch Screen Computer Kiosk, or Career America Connection.   ○
INS or U.S. Border Patrol's internet web sites.   ○
OPM's USAJOBS internet web site.   ○
Other internet web sites.   ○
State Employment Office.   ○
Job announcement on DOD Transition Bulletin Board.   ○
Exiting military personnel job fair.   ○
Other job fairs.   ○
Other sources.   ○

We request the following information in order to evaluate our efforts to recruit minorities and women. Providing this information is voluntary. This information will not be use to make selections nor will your chances for employment be affected if you do not answer these questions. Additionally, we treat the information that you provide to us as confidential, and we protect it from disclosure under the Privacy Act at 5 U.S.C. Section 552a(b). OMB Clearance Number 1115-0188, Expiration Date October 31, 1999.

A. Gender

   ○ Male   ○ Female

B. National Origin

   Are you of Hispanic/Latino Origin?   ○ Yes ○ No

FIGURE 8-1
Portion of the Border Patrol agent application form available online. You may complete the form online and submit it via the Net.

to succeed in that field, what other majors, minors, and non-CJ courses may be useful to take, where to find and obtain research data on crime and justice, and links to a variety of issues and important sites related to criminal justice.

The section titled "Life After Graduation" offers users information on careers in criminal justice—including descriptions of many of them, search engines for finding job openings, links to professional associations, and a dynamic site on graduate study. If you're anticipating graduate study, be sure to visit this site! Links to every graduate criminal justice or criminology program in the U. S. are provided along with insights on choosing thesis and dissertation topics, a degree committee, how to negotiate one's salary (for academics), and some of the insider information about how someone earns tenure and gets promoted.

Included in the "Life After Graduation" section are links to a variety of grant and funding agencies that specialize in supporting non-profit efforts— particularly useful information for criminal justice graduates who end up working for non-profit organizations.

Unlike most advising situations, students are able to access this online advisor, complete with e-mail contact, 24 hours a day, 365 days a year. Because it is maintained on a regular basis, the advice and insights offered are up-to-date and timely. Information on the site is written in a style that is inviting and positive— it draws users into thinking about what they are doing at the university and how their college time may best be spent.

AdviseNet© was created in 1996 by Dr. Mike Carlie, Professor of Sociology and Criminal Justice at Southwest Missouri State University, and is regularly updated by him. Dr. Carlie has been teaching, conducting research, publishing, and serving the professional community since receiving his Ph.D. in Sociology from Washington University (St. Louis) in 1970. He served on the Criminal Justice Planning Agency, U. S. Department of Justice, and on numerous community boards as a member and as an executive. He has been an intern supervisor and has been influential in the creation of several different university-level criminal justice programs since 1972. These experiences, and knowledge gained from having had over 25,000 students in his classroom over the years, inform the site and assure the user of realistic advice. Check out Dr. Carlie's vitae on AdviseNet©.

A similar, although generic, site is Prentice Hall Publishing Company's Student Success Supersite (http://www.prenhall.com/success). The Prentice Hall site offers majors exploration, career advice, student bulletin boards, faculty resources, tips from successful students, and many useful Web links.

JOB LISTING SERVICES

This chapter presents job listing services in four categories: (1) general listing services, (2) government-run or government-sponsored job sites, (3) criminal-justice-specific job listing services, and (4) state job listings. We'll start with general listing services.

~ AdviseNet ~

The On-Line Criminal Justice Advisor

With Dr. Mike Carlie
Department of Sociology and Anthropology
Southwest Missouri State University
Springfield, MO
TEL.: (417) 836-5642   FAX: (417) 836-6416

Click here for the story behind the picture.

What do you think of AdviseNet?

© 1996 Michael Kaye Carlie

Acknowledgements: Thank you to Dr. Marvin Prosono,
Jerome J. Malone, and Matt Cook for their technical
assistance in the early stages in the development of
AdviseNet.
Disclaimer: A link from **AdviseNet** to another site on the
Internet does not represent an endorsement of that site nor
guarantee the accuracy or approve of what may be seen or
heard at that site.

How to Search on the Internet

Getting Started
What is AdviseNet?
Dr. Carlie's Vita
Advisee Questionnaire
Check Class Availability
Admissions & Financial Aid
Get Better Grades in College
How to Succeed in College
How to Use the General Ed.
Requirement to Your Advantage

Studying Criminal Justice
The CJ Major and Minor
Non-CJ Courses for CJ Students
Other Degrees for CJ Students
Programs
Programs and Events
Research in Criminal Justice
Issues and Cool Sites
The CJSociety (Student Club)
Resource Pages for My Courses

Life After Graduation
Careers in Criminal Justice
Professional Associations
Graduate Study
Grant Opportunities
Financial Advise
Search Engines
Looking for Something To Do?

To CAS Homepage / SMSU / E-mail Dr Carlie / Career Day

Other sites created by Dr. Carlie
Kid Central and Southwest Missouri Interagency Task Force on Gangs and Youth Violence

FIGURE 8-2

The home page of Dr. Carlie's AdviseNet—a site dedicated to helping crimi-
nal justice students find fulfilling careers.
Screenshot courtesy of Dr. Carlie, Department of Sociology and Anthropology, Southwest Missouri
State University.

General Job Listing Services

General job listing services frequently provide up-to-date information on positions that are available *now*. They are a lot like "help wanted" sections in newspapers or trade journals. Some sites, however, provide much more—including
resume-posting services, career development guides, tuition assistance information, and so on.

Among the most useful sites are those which allow employers to search for
potential employees. If you are seeking employment, many of these sites help you
prepare a resume, advise you on how to submit it to agencies that are currently
hiring, or list your resume and credentials online for potential employers to see.
You may want to consider posting your own resume online and then directing

potential employers to it. Doing so can demonstrate your technical and computer prowess. You can view the online resume of Dr. Schmalleger, Director of the Justice Research Association online at http://cjcentral.com/resume. Although it is unlikely that your resume will be nearly as lengthy as Dr. Schmalleger's, this page should give you an idea of how to build your own online resume.

Some of the best general listing job services include the following (note: most services are free, but you may have to first register online or join the sponsoring agency or association to gain full access to some sites):

4Work   http://www.4work.com

Allows you to screen thousands of Web-posted jobs to find the one that's right for you. Job Alert!, a special feature of the site, is a confidential job search agent that screens thousands of jobs. You get results in approximately two minutes with fresh updates sent to your e-mail box daily. Searches are free for job seekers.

Career Builder   http://careerbuilder.com

This site provides a great job search feature that allows potential employees to search using criteria like salary, geographic region, type of job sought, and key words.

Career Magazine   http://www.careermag.com

A comprehensive resource designed to meet the individual needs of networked job seekers. More than just a job search site, Career Magazine is just what its name implies—a Web-based e-magazine for job seekers and employers.

Career Mosaic   http://www.careermosaic.com

One of the oldest search sites on the Web, Career Mosaic allows job seekers to search according to a wide range of criteria and to receive e-mail notification when jobs of potential interest are posted to the site.

Careernet   http://www.careers.org

A listing of over 11,000 links to jobs, employers, business, education, and career service professionals and over 6,000 links to employment-related resources.

Careersite   http://www.careersite.com

A free service that permits employers to submit want ads to many different job boards. The site also serves as a tool to help employers manage responses. Job seekers can post confidential resumes at the site.

CareerMart   http://www.careermart.com

CareerMart bills itself as "the most user-friendly employment site on the Web." With only a few clicks you can find job listings in your area of interest.

CareerPath   http://www.careerpath.com

CareerPath provides users with access to thousands of job ads scanned from hundreds of newspapers across the country.

Careerweb   http://www.cweb.com

A free place to store your resume online. Uses a job-match function to track your targeted job preferences with e-mail notification.

College Grad Job Hunter   http://www.collegegrad.com

Featured sections provide information preparing for a career and preparing for the job interview, writing a resume and cover letter, and negotiating a salary. Job postings and resume postings are available.

Cool Works   http://www.coolworks.com/showme

The site says that you can "live and work where others only visit." It lists 75,000 jobs in places like national parks, camps, resorts, amusement parks, ski resorts, and state parks. Many of the listings are for seasonal employment.

HeadHunter.net   http://www.headhunter.net

Although most general job search sites charge employers to post ads, HeadHunter is totally free to both employers and employees. Both ads and resumes, however, can be upgraded and made more visible for a fee.

Hot Jobs   http://www.hotjobs.com

Organized by category, the site provides lots of listings, including jobs in Canada, Australia, and elsewhere. You can search by keyword, company, or location.

Intellimatch   http://www.intellimatch.com

Matches your resume with the needs of prospective employers.

JobDirect   http://www.jobdirect.com

A site that focuses on linking college students and college graduates with potential employers. JobDirect TV streams video featuring potential employers to your desktop.

Job-Hunt   http://www.job-hunt.org

Offers specialized job listings, including those in academic, computers, engineering, accounting, consulting, medicine, and so on. Visit the site's "Law and Law Enforcement" section at http://www.job-hunt.org/law.shtml.

Jobtrack   http://www.jobtrak.com

A job-listing service that partners with hundreds of college and university career centers. It is used by over 200,000 employers.

JobWeb   http://www.jobweb.org

This site offers lots of job-hunting tips, along with an employment outlook and an "online career fair."

Jobs.com   http://www.jobs.com

Find employment by zip code, category, or keywords. The site provides a wealth of career resources, including a resume writing tool and message boards.

The Monster Board   http://www.monster.com

PC Magazine (the May 25, 1999 issue) rates Monster.com the best online site for both job seekers and employers. The "My Monster" personalization feature is highly customizable and allows job seekers to create a number of resumes, cover letters, and job-search agents.

The Riley Guide   http://www.dbm.com/jobguide

A very comprehensive job seeker's site with lots of links to related services. Last time we checked, however, the interface was from the Web's stone age.

Government Job Sites

America's Job Bank   http://www.ajb.dni.us

A totally free site, with a good resume creation facility, job market information, and a powerful job search engine. Run by the U. S. Department of Labor, the site hosts nearly 1 million job listings. The site hosts a national database of resumes in an area called America's Talent Bank.

Database of Government Jobs
http://www.govtjobs.com/crim/index.html

One of the latest and most up-to-date listings of state and federal government job opportunities. This a private (non-government-run) site that also provides job resource information by state.

Special Agent Employment/Vacancies

Special Agent Employment/Vacancies

Support Employment/ Vacancies

Internship Programs

Benefits

Policies & Practices

FBI Headquarters Divisions & Offices

Career Fairs

Privacy & Security Notice

Employment Home Page

FBI Home Page

| General Information | First Assignment | Entry Requirements | Advancement | Application Process |

General Information

Law Enforcement At Its Best

Since its founding in 1908 as the Bureau of Investigation, the FBI has evolved into one of the most respected and sophisticated law enforcement agencies in the world. As the primary investigative arm of the federal government, the FBI is responsible for enforcing over 260 federal statutes and for conducting sensitive national security investigations.

FBI activities include investigations into organized crime, white-collar crime, public corruption, financial crime, fraud against the government, bribery, copy-right matters, civil rights violations, bank robbery, extortion, kidnapping, air piracy, terrorism, foreign counterintelligence, interstate criminal activity, fugitive and drug-trafficking matters, and other violations of federal statutes.

The FBI also works with other federal, state and local law enforcement agencies in investigating matters of joint interest and in training law enforcement officers at the FBI Academy.

FIGURE 8-3
Want to be an FBI special agent? Check out the FBI's employment page on the Web at http://www.fbi.gov/employment/agent.htm.

Department of Labor Employment and Training Administration   http://www.doleta.gov

FBI Personnel and Employment Page
http://www.fbi.gov/employment/agent.htm

Information on hiring, recruitment, salaries, and employment statistics. Figure 8-3 shows the opening page for FBI employment information.

FedWorld Jobs   http://www.fedworld.gov/jobs/jobsearch.html

This Web site contains a series of database files using input from hundreds of human resources people in the federal government. The database allows you to search abstracts of open U. S. federal government jobs, and it is updated every Tuesday through Saturday at 9:30 A.M. EST.

FIGURE 8-4
The USA Jobs home page at http://www.usajobs.opm.gov. This government-run site lists thousands of jobs across the country, many of them in the criminal justice area.

Federal Support Services
http://www.federalsupportservices.com/fssframe.html

This site tells visitors that the federal government employs approximately 100,000 law enforcement personnel and hires *hundreds*, even *thousands*, of personnel each year! Unfortunately, the site provides little help to job seekers beyond attempting to sell visitors printed packages to assist them in job searches. It does, however, contain links to a number of other useful sites.

USA Jobs   http://www.usajobs.opm.gov

The United States Office of Personnel Management runs a *huge* jobs Web site at this address. All kinds of jobs are listed, but a search feature makes it possible to easily find jobs in the criminal justice area. Online applications are also available. The site's opening page is shown in Figure 8-4.

Criminal Justice Job Listing Services

Criminal justice-specific job listing services come in two flavors: (1) general and (2) agency or area specific. The following list describes both kinds of services:

Corrections Jobs   http://www.corrections.com/jobs

The Corrections Connection job-listing service.

Dr. Carlie's AdviseNet
http://www.smsu.edu/contrib/soc/advnet/advnet.htm

A new concept in online advising for criminal justice students. Provides users with advice on where the field is going, where to find jobs (includes many job search engines), and additional useful information for students at *any* university. The site is maintained by Dr. Mike Carlie of Southwest Missouri State University, and was discussed in greater detail earlier in this chapter.

Ira Wilsker's Law Enforcement Employment Page
http://www.ih2000.net/ira/ira2.htm#jobs

An excellent, information-rich, jobs page!

Law Enforcement Careers   http://www.gate.net/fcfjobs

A full-service career site for those seeking employment in the law enforcement field. Law Enforcement Careers categorizes job information as follows: (1) Federal Law Enforcement Careers, (2) State Trooper Careers, and (3) Correctional Officer Careers. The site also provides separate testing guides, including the "Federal Law Enforcement Testing Guide" and the "State and Local Law Enforcement Testing Guide."

Law Enforcement Jobs   http://www.lawenforcementjobs.com

This may be the best site on the Web for anyone looking for employment in the law enforcement field. The site lists jobs with local departments, state departments, federal agencies, the U. S. military, private security, associations, and schools. A training calendar adds a nice touch. The site is free to job seekers, and allows you to post a resume and cover letter online and manage your search online with a Job Seeker Account. Resumes, which can be easily edited, stay in the database until you delete them.

National Directory of Emergency Services
http://www1.policejobs.com/ndes/phome.html

An up-to-the-minute source for police department employment opportunities.

Police Careers   http://www.policecareer.com/employment.html

A professional police resume and career service company.

Police Employment   http://www.policeemployment.com

This site provides information on careers in law enforcement and corrections, and offers visitors the opportunity to purchase law enforcement testing guides, videos, and police interview guides. A jobs page shows "who is hiring."

The Police Officers' Internet Directory Jobs Page
http://www.officer.com/jobs.htm

A very comprehensive listing of current law enforcement jobs. Highly recommended for those seeking law enforcement employment.

Police Jobs   http://www.tap.net/hyslo/poljobs.htm

Extensive list of police employment sites.

The Public Safety Executive Association (PSEA)
http://www.policechief.com/default.htm

A membership site that helps members who are beginning careers in the field of public safety.

Public Safety Recruitment   http://www.psrjobs.com/lawrecru.htm

Established in 1993 to help students and peace officers reach their law enforcement career goals, PSR provides information from thousands of paid law enforcement agencies from across the nation.

The State Police Information Center
http://www.internetwks.com/officers

A nationwide provider of state and federal law enforcement career information. The interface for this site may be a bit tricky.

State Job Listings

Although there is no stand-alone listing of criminal justice-related jobs at the state level available on the Web (yet!) there are a number of places you can go to find up-to-date listings in corrections, law enforcement, and the law. One such place is the COP-SPOT employment page, which you can visit at http://www.cop-spot.com /employment/links.html. Another useful page on the COP-SPOT site runs at http://www.cop-spot.com/employment/jobs.html. For a listing of many other criminal-justice-specific job sites, visit the University of North Texas' Employment Opportunities site at http://www.unt.edu/cjus/employ.htm. Finally, don't forget Law Enforcement Jobs, mentioned earlier in this chapter (http://www.lawenforcementjobs.com). It, too, contains many state-specific listings.

If you are uncertain whether you want to enter the law enforcement profession, you can see what it is like to attend a police academy in cyberspace by visiting *The New Blue Line*. *The New Blue Line* traces an officer's steps through the Virginia Beach, Virginia, Police Academy from the day of arrival through graduation. The project is the work of *Virginian-Pilot* reporter Mike Mather, who attended the academy to see what it would be like and then wrote about his experiences. The newspaper describes the resulting online experience this way: "Spend five months inside the Virginia Beach Police Academy. Follow three recruits as they face the grueling physical regimen, the nerve-wracking firing-range test…and the terror of The Redman. Two recruits will survive. One will fail. Would you?" The site makes for an interesting experience! *The New Blue Line* can be reached at http://www.pilotonline.com/special/blueline.

USING THE WEB

Visit some of the job sites described in this chapter. Once there, search for jobs in the area of law enforcement. Look for jobs in corrections. Then answer the following questions:

1. Which sites did you visit? What made you choose those sites?
2. Which site do you consider to be the best for job searches? Why?
3. What search terms did you use? Are there other, alternative, terms that you might have used? If so, what are they?
4. If you were seeking employment in one of these fields (police work or corrections), which three of the jobs you found listed would you apply for? What makes those jobs attractive?

9

Security Issues

As surely as the future will bring new forms of technology, it will bring new forms of crime.

—*Cynthia Mason and Charles Ardai*[30]

Thou shalt not steal thy neighbor's data.

—*InterLock® security devices advertisement*

CHAPTER OUTLINE

Security on the Internet

Security Information

Viruses

Antivirus Sites and Information

Using the Web

SECURITY ON THE INTERNET

You have probably heard quite a bit about security on the Internet. Security is important because there are a number of unscrupulous people (sometimes called *crackers* because they work to crack codes, passwords, etc.), well versed in technology, who spend time and money trying to steal personal information from other Internet users. Such high-tech criminals often try to grab passwords, credit card numbers, personal banking information, and other types of valuable data (including business plans for new products, government plans for military action, etc.) from the Internet. They do so by using their computers and special software to secretly enter Internet information pipelines. Then they watch the flow of information along those pipelines, looking for valuable data that is unencrypted.

One of the most basic types of security about which you should be concerned involves keeping your password a secret. If others acquire your password, they can use it to masquerade as you, enter your Internet or online account, and leave you with the bill for their online activities. Worse, once they have logged on as you, they can change your password—effectively locking you out of your own accounts!

You can protect your password by remembering a few basic tips:

>> Do not share your password with *anyone*. Of course you have trusted friends. But even trusted friends may inadvertently share information with others, while some may not be as dependable as you thought. You should be especially attentive to the need to keep your password private while you are online. *Never* give your password to anyone who sends you an e-mail message asking for it unless you are sure you know the requester. Even then, if you e-mail a password to a trusted friend, your e-mail message could be intercepted by a cracker sitting on an Internet node looking for just such information. Members of the America Online service, for example, sometimes receive "instant messages" (IMs) from other members masquerading as system administrators for AOL. Those fraudulent IMs sometimes request passwords and other personal information. Although AOL has worked hard to eliminate this security problem, it is still occurring at the time of this writing.

>> Do not write your password for online access or online accounts in any place that is easily visible. One person at the Justice Research Association, for example, got into the habit of writing her password on yellow sticky tabs, which she then posted on the edges of her computer monitor. While it may be okay to use sticky tabs to remind you of your mother's birthday, it is *not* a good idea to paste tabs containing passwords anywhere they can be seen by others.

>> Change your password on a regular basis. Some people recommend changing your password every month; others suggest every six months. The point to keep in mind is that the longer you use the same password, the more likely it is to be "broken" or to fall into the hands of an unscrupulous person. Crackers may be trying to break your password without your knowledge by using software to contact your ISP or online service repeatedly, each time randomly trying a computer-generated password and waiting until the system lets them in.

>> Use a password that is at least eight characters long and that is made up of a mix of letters and numbers.

>> Do not use a password that someone who knows you could easily guess (like the name of your dog or cat or the name of your boyfriend or girlfriend).

>> Do not use an English-language word as your password. Given the technology available to crackers, they are the easiest passwords to break.

>> Do not allow anyone to watch as you type in your password. This is the most common way that passwords are compromised.

>> Do not use your username or user ID as your password. Both are required to log on, and many people ask, "Why remember two words when I can type the same one in twice?" People who receive e-mail from you may be able to learn your username or ID, and they may try using it as your password.

>> Do *not* use well-known abbreviations, names of fictional characters, or names of television or movie heroes or heroines.

Given all this advice on what *not* to use as a password, what *should* you use? Some people suggest using a sentence that is easy to remember and then creating a password based on that sentence. For example, "My daughter is four years old" is easy to remember and can be used as the basis for a password like "mdis4yrold." Another password might come from the sentence, "The Justice Research Association was created in 1978" (jrain1978). In case you are wondering, no, we don't use that password at the Justice Research Association.

Whether you follow this advice or not, if you notice that strange things are happening with your account you should contact your ISP or online service immediately. *And* you should immediately change your password.

Beyond passwords, there are other security issues of which you should be aware. Most of today's popular browsers have a number of important security features built in. In order to use many of them, however, you must be connected to a site that runs on a secure server, or you must have **security certificates** installed on your own computer. A *security certificate* is a file that electronically identifies a person or an organization. Browsers use certificates to encrypt information. You can use a certificate to check the identity of the certificate's owner. You should trust a certificate only if you trust the person or organization that issued it.

Some sites run on secure servers, which will automatically encrypt any information you send back to them via an HTML form. An HTML form is a Web page sent to you by the secure server that you can fill out and send back to that same server. Secure servers make it possible for you to engage in secure transactions and to exchange information over the Web without the need for any special security software on your own machine. Forms sent to you by secure servers usually contain wording that looks something like this: "First, click here to activate SSL [Secure Sockets Layer] protocol. All of the information you will enter will then be securely transferred using RSA encryption." Rather than RSA encryption,[31] they might refer to DES (Data Encryption Standard) security or some other form of encryption security, or simply tell you that the HTML form you are working with is a secure document. Another way to tell if you are sending information in a secure mode initiated by the server you are in contact with is to look at the URL in your browser's location field. Secure connections will usually be indicated by the preface "https://" rather than the usual "http://."

> **Data encryption:** methods used to encode computerized information, making the data inaccessible to unauthorized individuals.

You can also set your browser to alert you if you are about to send sensitive information to a nonsecure site or if you are about to send sensitive information that is not encrypted. Communicator, for example, pops up a box labeled "SECURITY WARNING," that says "You have requested a secure document. The document and any information you send back are encrypted for privacy while in transit." Encrypted information can be read only by someone who has a decryption key, such as a password that you provide to them. Most browsers set the alert to display by default. You can disable alerts by choosing the "options" or "preferences" selections in your browser, finding the security section, and clicking on the checkbox "display security warnings" (or similar wording). Clicking on the checkbox should remove the existing checkmark, thus disabling the warnings.

Even if alerts are not set to be displayed, most browsers make it easy to tell if you are sending or receiving information from a secure site (such as a banking institution that makes your personal financial files available to you online). Both Netscape Communicator and Internet Explorer display a padlock on the bottom right of the window in which they appear, indicating that you are operating in a secure mode.

Communicator categorizes security certificates into four groups: (1) Yours (your own certificates), (2) People (certificates sent to you from other people or organizations), (3) Web Sites (certificates sent to you from Web sites), and (4)

Signers (certificates from certificate signers, also known as "Certificate Authorities").

One especially important provider of digital authentication products and services is VeriSign Corporation. As the first commercial Certificate Authority, VeriSign has issued Digital IDs for almost every secure Internet server worldwide. Strict verification and security practices, enforced through automated background checks and state-of-the-art security systems, ensure the integrity of every VeriSign Digital ID. Visit the VeriSign Digital ID issuing center at http://www.verisign.com/idcenter/new/idplus.html for additional information.

While space does not permit discussion of all the potential security issues involved in use of the Internet, the following letter from Senator Patrick Leahy (D-VT) indicates the growing importance of this issue. The letter was sent by Senator Leahy to various organizations and mailing list forums, including the Electronic Frontier Foundation's "ACTION" list.

From: Senator_Leahy@leahy.senate.gov

Date: May 2, 1996, 12:02:02 EST

Subject: Letter From Senator Patrick Leahy (D-VT) On Encryption

To: action@eff.org (action mailing list) Please post where appropriate

————BEGIN PRETTY GOOD PRIVACY SIGNED MESSAGE————

Dear Friends:

Today, a bipartisan group of Senators has joined me in supporting legislation to encourage the development and use of strong, privacy-enhancing technologies for the Internet by rolling back the out-dated restrictions on the export of strong cryptography. In an effort to demonstrate one of the more practical uses of encryption technology (and so that you all know this message actually came from me), I have signed this message using a digital signature generated by the popular encryption program PGP [Pretty Good Privacy].

I am proud to be the first member of Congress to utilize encryption and digital signatures to post a message to the Internet. As a fellow Internet user, I care deeply about protecting individual privacy and encouraging the development of the Net as a secure and trusted communications medium. I do not need to tell you that current export restrictions only allow American companies to export primarily weak encryption technology.

The current strength of encryption the U.S. government will allow out of the country is so weak that, according to a January 1996 study conducted by world-renowned cryptographers, a pedestrian hacker can crack the codes in a matter of hours! A foreign intelligence agency can crack the current 40-bit codes in seconds.

Perhaps more importantly, the increasing use of the Internet and similar interactive communications technologies by Americans to obtain critical medical services, to conduct business, to be entertained and communicate with their friends, raises special concerns about the privacy and confidentiality of those communications.

I have long been concerned about these issues, and have worked over the past decade to protect privacy and security for our wire and electronic communications. Encryption technology provides an effective way to ensure that only the people we choose can read our communications. I have read horror stories sent to me over the Internet about how human rights groups in the Balkans have had their computers confiscated during raids by security police seeking to find out the identities of people who have complained about abuses.

Thanks to PGP, the encrypted files were undecipherable by the police and the names of the people who entrusted their lives to the human rights groups were safe. The new bill, called the "Promotion of Commerce online in the Digital Era (PRO-CODE) Act of 1996," would: (1) bar any government-mandated use of any particular encryption system, including key escrow systems, and affirm the right of American citizens to use whatever form of encryption they choose domestically; (2) loosen export restrictions on encryption products so that American companies are able to export any generally available or mass market encryption products without obtaining government approval; and (3) limit the authority of the federal government to set standards for encryption products used by businesses and individuals, particularly standards which result in products with limited key lengths and key escrow.

This is the second encryption bill I have introduced with Senator Burns and other congressional colleagues this year. Both bills call for an overhaul of this country's export restrictions on encryption, and, if enacted, would quickly result in the widespread availability of strong, privacy protecting technologies. Both bills also prohibit a government-mandated key escrow encryption system. While PRO-CODE would limit the authority of the Commerce Department to set encryption standards for use by private individuals and businesses, the first bill we introduced, called the "Encrypted Communications Privacy Act," S.1587, would set up stringent procedures for law enforcement to follow to obtain decoding keys or decryption assistance to read the plain text of encrypted communications obtained under court order or other lawful process. It is clear that the current policy towards encryption exports is hopelessly outdated, and fails to account for the real needs of individuals and businesses in the global marketplace. Encryption expert Matt Blaze, in a recent letter to me, noted that current U.S. regulations governing the use and export of encryption are having a "deleterious effect...on our country's ability to develop a reliable and trustworthy information infrastructure." The time is right for Congress to take steps to put our national encryption policy on the right course. I am looking forward to hearing from you on this important issue. Throughout the course of the recent debate on the Communications Decency Act, the input from Internet users was very valuable to me and some of my Senate colleagues. You can find out more about the issue at my World Wide Web homepage (http://www.leahy.senate.gov) [if this address does not work, try http://www.senate.gov/member/vt/leahy/general or http://www.senate.gov/leahy] and at the Encryption Policy Resource Page (http://www.crypto.com). Over the coming months, I look forward to the help of the Net community in convincing other Members of Congress and the Administration of the need to reform our nation's cryptography policy.

Sincerely,

Patrick Leahy
United States Senator

If you want to learn more about Internet security, you should visit the Computer Security Institute (http://www.gocsi.com), or you can go to the Computer Emergency Response Team (CERT®) Coordination Center at http://www.cert.org. The CERT Coordination Center, located at Carnegie Mellon University in Pittsburgh, Pennsylvania, studies Internet security vulnerabilities, provides incident response services to sites that have been the victims of attack, publishes a variety of security alerts, researches security and survivability in wide-area-networked computing, and develops information to help Web developers improve security at your site.[32]

Another excellent source of Web security information is the World Wide Web Security FAQ (Frequently Asked Questions) site at http://www.w3. org/Security/Faq. You might also check out the home page of Pretty Good Privacy (PGP) software at http://www.pgp.com. PGP allows you to encode your e-mail and protect its contents against prying eyes anywhere on the Net. PGP also allows you to encrypt and decrypt files that are stored on your own computer to prevent others from accessing them. PGP freeware (for use only within the United States) can be found at http://web.mit.edu/network/pgp.html and at the PGP Web site. If you visit the PGP site, you will see this reminder: "Please remember that all cryptographic software is classified as export-controlled by the U. S. Department of Commerce. If you are a citizen of the USA or Canada, or have permanent alien resident status in the United States, you may legally purchase and download the software." The same restrictions apply to PGP freeware.

It is not our purpose to discuss Net security in great detail in this short guide. If you are interested in further study, you might review some of the sources for information on Net security that follow. Keep in mind that some of the information found at these sites can be very technical. Other sites contain primarily political information (that is, arguments for and against the use of various forms of data security).

SECURITY COMPANIES AND RELATED SITES

The CERT Coordination Center   http://www.cert.org

The CERT home page. CERT focuses on computer security concerns for Internet users.

Computer Security Awareness
http://www.hhs.net/dpec/courses/sec/sectitle.htm

A rich interactive learning experience focused on computer security.

Computer Security Institute (CSI)   http://www.gocsi.com

CSI, which has been in operation since 1974, is the world's leading membership organization specifically dedicated to serving and training the information, computer, and network security professional.

CyberCrime.gov   http://www.cybercrime.gov

A U. S. Government site that provides information about computer crimes, with sections on policy, cases, laws, and documents. Information on how to report computer crimes is included. A free newsletter is available through the site.

Computer Security News Daily   http://www.mountainwave.com

A great site for those seeking up-to-the-minute computer security news. News is available in the following categories: government, business, development, hacks and cracks, the Net, law, and international.

Electronic Frontier Foundation (EFF)   http://www.eff.org

The Electronic Frontier Foundation is the civil liberties union of cyberspace.

Electronic Privacy Information Center (EPIC)   http://epic.org

EPIC, the Electronic Privacy Information Center, is a public interest research center in Washington, D.C. It was established in 1994 to focus public attention on emerging civil liberties issues and to protect privacy, the First Amendment, and constitutional values.

Entrust Technologies   http://www.entrust.com

Entrust Technologies develops software security products for encryption and digital signature. Its home page provides links to product information, a resource library, company press releases, partners, events, FAQs, and Web security references.

International Cryptography   http://www.ssh.com/tech/crypto

A site listing international sources of cryptographic software, information on cryptographic methods, algorithms, and protocols. Materials cover encryption, decryption, cryptanalysis, steganography (hiding information), software, tools, information, and assessments about cryptographic methods.

International Pretty Good Privacy (PGP) Home Page
http://www.pgpi.com

Provides up-to-date information about PGP, FAQs, bugs, documentation, and links regarding the latest international PGP versions.

Network Security Buyer's Guide
http://www.netsecurityguide.com

Provides information about network security, utilities, and virus protection. Offers a searchable database of products, links to vendor sites, and a library of white papers, press releases, and product presentations.

Journal of Computer Security   http://www2.csl.sri.com/jcs

The journal presents research and development results in the theory, design, implementation, analysis and application of secure computer systems and networks. Unfortunately, full-text articles are not available online.

National Institute of Standards and Technology Computer Security Resource Clearinghouse http://csrc.nist.gov/welcome.html

NIST's computer security resource clearinghouse contains information on numerous security topics, as well as alerts about viruses and other security threats.

PBS Safe Computing Library
http://www.pbs.org/wgbh/pages/frontline/shows/hackers/vigilant

Includes great (and very readable) articles on safe surfing, cookies, what to do if you've been hacked, and using privacy tools.

PC Privacy   http://www.pcprivacycentral.com

A commercial site that offers products and advice to make your PC private and secure. The PC Privacy Protection Program Guide is available free at http://www.pcprivacycentral.com/pcprivacy.doc.

Quadralay's Cryptography Archive
http://www.austinlinks.com/Crypto

This archive is a collection of links relating to electronic privacy and cryptography.

RSA Data Security   http://www.rsa.com

Site of RSA Data Security, Inc., creators of the RSA encryption technology used in Netscape Communicator, Quicken, Lotus Notes, and hundreds of other products.

Secure Root   http://www.secureroot.com

The site provides information on cyberlaw, encryption, hacking, security, phreaking, cracking, Internet anonymity, and lots of other topics. Links to dozens of computer security 'Zines are provided.

University of California at Davis Computer Security Laboratory   http://seclab.cs.ucdavis.edu

The site provides a wealth of information on security under its "projects" and "papers" sections. Be forewarned: these are mostly highly technical documents that require considerable background in computer technology. NSA has designated the site a "Center of Academic Excellence in Information Assurance Education."

University of Toronto's Computer Security Administration
http://www.infocommons.utoronto.ca/security

Includes links to security organizations, security products, security news, alerts, and information on conferences, seminars, and training.

Verisign Corporation   http://www.verisign.com

The world leader in encryption technologies for individual and commercial use. See Verisign's secure e-mail reference guide at http://www.verisign.com/support/csh/help/index.htm. It explains the nature of digital IDs and what you can do with them.

VIRUSES

One of the perils of surfing the Web is the possibility that your computer (or your network, if your machine is connected to one) may become infected by computer viruses. A virus is a malicious and generally quite small software program designed and written to adversely affect your computer by altering the way it works without your knowledge or permission.[33] Viruses work secretly by implanting themselves into one or more of your files and then spreading quietly from one file to another when the originally infected file is accessed or read. They are written by human beings, *not* by computers, and are apparently intended to demonstrate the code writer's skills.

> **Virus:** a malicious and generally quite small software program designed and written to adversely affect your computer by altering the way it works without your knowledge or permission.

The reason that viruses are so called is that they have the ability to self-replicate and to propagate within one computer and across networks (like the Internet). Viruses often lurk in memory, waiting to infect the next program that is run or the next disk that is accessed.

Virus infections can come from a number of different sources, but the most common are shared disks (floppy or otherwise), the Internet, and infected computers on local area networks (LANs).

A few years ago viruses could be attached only to executable programs (those that actually run on your machine). Newer viruses, however, are much more insidious. Some, called **macro viruses**, including the **concept virus**, can attach themselves to Microsoft Word® files. Others can make their way into your computer through small programs called *scripts* that are downloaded to your machine while you browse the Web. Some of the most recent viral codes have been found hidden within Java scripts, ActiveX applets, and Shockwave programs—small scripts written by Web site designers to provide motion and interactivity on their Web sites. **Cookies**, small programs that are sent to your machine by sites you visit, may also contain viruses.

> **Cookies:** The collective name for files stored on your hard drive by your Web browser that hold information about your browsing habits (which sites you have visited, which newsgroups you have read, etc.). Cookies are sent to your computer by sites that you visit.

Viruses may activate immediately upon download, or may be set to activate on a certain date (such as the Michelangelo virus, which runs when your computer's internal clock reaches the artist's birth date). They may also activate after a certain period of time or during a given activity, called a *trigger*, performed by the user. A trigger may be something as simple as attempting to save a certain kind of file. The important thing to realize is that you can easily download a virus off the Web without being aware of it. Once that happens, the virus will patiently wait in your computer until the conditions specified by the program's author manifest themselves.

Some viruses are relatively harmless and do little more than take over the computer screen in order to display a leering graphic or a phrase like "gotcha." These are called **benign viruses**. Others, called **malignant viruses**, are more insidious and can cause letters and words on your screen to crumble or fall to pieces. The worst of the malignant viruses can corrupt selected files, delete important operating files from your disk, fill up your hard drives and computer memory (thereby slowing your machine to a crawl), or reformat your entire hard disk—destroying all of the information in your computer or making it inaccessible to you.[34]

Viruses fall into four general categories, depending on how they work inside your machine. The first are **file infectors**. These are viruses that attach themselves to, or replace, **executable files** with name extensions like "COM," "EXE," "SYS," "DRV," "BIN," or "OVL." The file that runs Windows, for example, is called "windows.com," and has been a frequent target of virus writers.

> **Executable files:** program files that actually run on your machine and generally do not change in size, as opposed to text, document, or data files, which are routinely modified as you work with them.

A second viral category is that of **boot sector infectors**. Boot sector infectors work by attacking the boot sector on floppy disks or hard drives. (They may also infect removable storage media, such as Iomega Zip® and Jaz® drives, although those types of drives are rarely used to boot machines.) All disks have a boot sector, even those that cannot be used to start, or boot, your machine. Boot sector viruses spread when users leave an infected diskette in a drive and attempt to boot or reboot their machines. Even though the disk may appear to be an empty floppy disk, when the machine attempts to boot, the first thing it will do is try to read and execute the boot sector. The virus is then read into the machine's memory and infects the hard drive. Although it is easy to acquire a boot sector infection, it is not easy to tell when it has occurred. Attempting to boot from an infected disk will result in the message, "Non-System Disk." Even though you may pop the infected floppy out of your floppy drive and proceed to boot normally from your hard drive, infection has already occurred.

A third category of viruses is called **master boot record infectors** (MBRIs). MBRIs infect what is called the *master boot program* on the hard drive(s) in your computer. Since your computer will read the boot program at startup time, it will also run whatever instructions are included in the MBRI virus. Finally, **multipartite viruses** comprise the fourth category of virus. They are simply a combination of two or more of the types already discussed.

Although not a separate category, it is important to realize that certain kinds of viruses, called *stealth viruses* and *polymorphic viruses*, are smart enough to change themselves slightly each time they infect a new machine. Because most antivirus programs depend largely on a database of known viruses (called a *virus signature file*) and compare files they find on your machine with known virus codes, polymorphic and stealth viruses can easily elude some of the best antivirus software available today. Many advanced antivirus programs, however, offer you the choice of inoculating the important files in your computer. The strategy behind inoculation is simple: The antivirus program simply records the size of the inoculated file (using only executable files that are not supposed to change), and periodically compares the recorded size with the current size of the file. Executable files that have changed in size are suspected of harboring a virus.

Antivirus Sites and Information

Antivirus Resources　http://www.hitchhikers.net/av.shtml

A wealth of online information about the virus problem, with access to recommended antivirus shareware and trial software.

Antivirus Encyclopedia　http://www.metro.ch/avpve

Anything you ever wanted to know about thousands of viruses—all in one place.

Dr. Solomon's Antivirus® Site　http://www.drsolomon.com

A comprehensive site with software, virus news, and listings of the most common viruses. Now a part of McAfee.com.

IBM Antivirus Research Site
http://www.research.ibm.com/antivirus

The site offers scientific papers, press releases, a virus time line and other information for many different operating systems. The time line (at http://www. research. ibm.com/antivirus/timeline.htm) is especially interesting.

McAfee Antivirus　http://www.mcafee.com

McAfee Antivirus is one of the most commonly used antivirus products on the market today. A "virus map" shows the location and number of infected files found worldwide in the past 24 hours—or any other time frame you specify.

Network Associates   http://www.nai.com

Network Associates is one of the major antivirus software vendors in the world. Trial versions of most of their products are available for free downloading. The site also provides a wealth of virus information.

New Mexico Highlands University's Computer Virus Information Page   http://jaring.nmhu.edu/virus.htm

Many different types of antivirus information. The site's motto is "Practice Safe Computing."

Sophos Antivirus Center   http://www.sophos.com

Includes a virus encyclopedia, virus hoaxes, antivirus software tools, and many other features.

Stiller Research   http://www.stiller.com/stiller.htm

The home of Integrity Master antivirus software. Includes lots of antivirus information.

Symantec Corporation's Antivirus® Center
http://www.symantec.com

Rated as one of the most comprehensive antivirus centers on the Web. The site is searchable by keyword. View current top threats at http://www.sarc.com.

Trend Micro Antivirus Products   http://www.antivirus.com

A Japanese antivirus company with lots of good information. Scan-mail antivirus software is available to protect your incoming e-mail messages.

USING THE WEB

Visit three of the antivirus sites described in this chapter. Once there, find the product descriptions for antivirus software available through these sites. Then answer the following questions:

1. Which sites did you visit? What made you choose those sites?
2. Compare the features of the antivirus products you found. How do they differ? How are they similar?
3. Which site offers the best antivirus software? Why do you think that particular product is the best?

10

Using the *Talk Justice* Site

Justice is Truth in action!

—*Benjamin Disraeli*

Injustice anywhere is a threat to justice everywhere!

—*M. L. King*

CHAPTER OUTLINE

THE PURPOSE OF THE SITE

A dedicated Web site supports this guide. Available 24 hours a day, the site is sponsored by the Justice Research Association with support from Prentice Hall Publishing Company. The name of the site is *Talk Justice*. You can reach *Talk Justice* by using this URL:

http://talkjustice.com

Talk Justice gives you the tools you need to keep up with the constantly changing world of URLs and the Internet. Visit *Talk Justice* for the latest Web addresses for sites discussed in this guide (and others), to access ongoing message boards focused on criminal justice issues (Figure 10-1 shows messages from the police

Conferences : Police : Police	
Discussion Topic	**Discussion Information**
police confessions and miranda as a result of miranda police have to warn individuals of their rights, such as their right to remain silent and the right to an attorney. Since polic...	Jennifer Feb-09-01 07:19 PM 1 messages
Is this a bribe? is it legal? Pulled over last night, 84 in a 65. cop told me to call him if I wanted to 'do something about making it go away'. I called him today to find out th...	Liam Feb-02-01 02:44 PM 2 messages
Police Mis-Conduct I am writing in search of Justice. I have been, and continue to be, the victim of police mis-conduct. My name is Raymond Dale Rhode, I am a Reserve...	Dale Rhode Jan-26-01 01:50 PM 0 messages
veterans preference hi. i am 19 years old. in 1 more year i will have an aa. in criminal justice. i was wondering what veterans preference does for an applicant, and how ...	matthew chetaitis Jan-23-01 12:58 PM 0 messages
weed laws? I was driving to work on friday nite. I had a small, "personal amount" of weed on me. I was pulled over for a faulty headlight. The officer walked up ...	Loadstorm Jan-20-01 07:01 PM 3 messages
BIG QUESTION* could determine weath... Ok, just wondering if anyone knows the proper procedure for an arrest. This cop arrested me for graffiti, he caught me in the act just as i finished u...	Albert Reo Jan-17-01 05:54 PM 6 messages
POLICE I live in a very small town. Only a Very Few of our officers know the LAW... *****SPECIAL NOTE***** I love all Animals..therefore, I do not Believe i...	KewlGranny Jan-13-01 11:08 AM 0 messages
About the Police Academy :) I am interested in Police Academy, but I don't know what classes should I take in the High School. I'm 10th grade right now, but since I was once in P...	Karina Jan-12-01 06:05 PM 8 messages

FIGURE 10-1

The police message boards on the *Talk Justice* site. Visit *Talk Justice* at http://www.talkjustice.com.

conference area on *Talk Justice*), and to participate in real-time chat with other *Talk Justice* users. Central features of the site include the following:

>> **Discussion Forums** *Talk Justice* discussion forums exist in the form of message boards. Once in the message area, you can search messages, browse message threads, or contribute your own new message(s).

>> **The Criminal Justice Image Map** The criminal justice image map is an innovative feature that diagrammatically represents processing through the criminal justice system. The map contains hot spots that lead to links for further exploring topical areas on the map. Try it! You'll like it!

>> **Real-Time Chat** The *Talk Justice* chat room allows you to join other *Talk Justice* users in a real-time chat area. Try the chat room at various times. Sometimes it is full of people chatting with one another, but at other times it is empty. If you find that you are the only person in the chat area, you might wait a few minutes and see if other people join you. Finally, remember that the Java-based chat facility takes a while to load on some computers (if you are behind a firewall that excludes Java applets from loading you won't be able to chat). The time required for the chat facility to load depends on the speed of your Internet connection and how busy the Net is. If you are working from a university computer center connected to a fast T1 line (or using an even faster T3 connection), you may not even notice the time it takes to enter the chat area. If you are connecting to *Talk Justice* through a modem, however, it may take up to two minutes for the chat feature to load, depending on your modem's speed.

>> **Rules for Posting on Talk Justice** *Talk Justice* began as a message-posting facility for those interested in criminal justice. It quickly became obvious, however, that not all posters respected other discussion group members. That made it necessary to institute rules for posting messages—which can be viewed by clicking on this hyperlink. The rules are not overly demanding. They are built on the netiquette principles discussed in Chapter 7 and ask mostly that you respect other *Talk Justice* users.

>> **The *Talk Justice* Cybrary** The Cybrary is an electronic library. It contains the kind of Web listings found in Chapter 3 of this guide. The Cybrary is constantly updated, ensuring that you will find the most current links available for the information you seek.

THE JUSTICE RESEARCH ASSOCIATION

A link on the *Talk Justice* home page takes you to the Justice Research Association (JRA), which sponsors the *Talk Justice* site. There you can learn about the association's involvement in distance learning. JRA sponsors the *Talk Justice* Web site and the Criminal Justice Distance Learning Consortium (CJDLC), and also supports efforts by colleges and universities to use the latest communications technology in the service of higher education in the criminal justice area.

Other activities undertaken by JRA include research in criminal justice, the creation and maintenance of Web sites relevant to criminal justice and criminology, and the ongoing development of a criminal justice Cybrary—a Web-based cyberlibrary with links to criminal justice sites throughout the world. You can reach JRA on the Web at http://www.cjcentral.com/jra. The JRA home page is shown in Figure 10-2.

FIGURE 10-2
The home page of the Justice Research Association, sponsors of the Criminal Justice Distance Learning Consortium (CJDLC), and Talk Justice.
Reprinted with permission.

THE CRIMINAL JUSTICE DISTANCE LEARNING CONSORTIUM

The Criminal Justice Distance Learning Consortium (CJDLC), which you can reach at http://cjcentral.com/cjdlc, provides resources to college and university criminal justice programs interested in distance learning. CJDLC facilitates distance education efforts through its online resource base, which includes links to Web sites supporting criminal justice distance learning technology. CJDLC also evaluates existing resources in support of teaching and is in the process of developing electronic classrooms for use by institutions lacking such facilities.

Membership in CJDLC is free and is open to both criminal justice instructors and institutions. Members receive a bimonthly e-newsletter, and they can have their e-mail addresses and links to their sites posted on the CJDLC site. CJDLC also provides a place for the electronic posting of articles and papers on distance learning. In this regard, CJDLC serves as a clearinghouse for information on distance learning in the criminal justice area. The CJDLC home page is shown in Figure 10-3.

FIGURE 10-3
The home page of the Criminal Justice Distance Learning Consortium (CJDLC). Visit CJDLC at http://cjcentral.com/cjdlc.
Reprinted with permission.

USING THE WEB

Visit the *Talk Justice* site at http://talkjustice.com. Once there, explore the site's features. Then answer the following questions:

1. What does this site have to offer? Provide a list of features available on *Talk Justice*.
2. How do the message boards differ from the chat area? Which did you find more useful? Why?
3. How do you think the *Talk Justice* site can best be used in your studies? Why?
4. Click on the "Distance Learning" link on the *Talk Justice* page. After visiting the Criminal Justice Distance Learning Consortium, describe what it offers.

Internet Glossary

This glossary is made available through the courtesy of SquareOne Technology and is reprinted with the permission of SquareOne. All rights are reserved by SquareOne Technology, http://www.squareonetech.com. Terms that have been added by the author to the SquareOne Glossary are indicated with an asterisk (*).

Add-in A miniprogram that runs in conjunction with a Web browser or other application that enhances the functionality of that program. In order for the add-in to run, the main application must be running as well.

Address The location of an Internet resource. An e-mail address may take the form of joeschmoe@somecompany.com. A Web address looks something like http://www.square-onetech.com.

Anchor Either the starting point or destination of a hyperlink. The letters at the top of this page are all anchors—clicking one takes you to another part of this page.

Anonymous FTP An anonymous FTP site allows Internet users to log in and download files from the computer without having a private userid and password. To log in, you typically enter anonymous as the userid and your e-mail address as the password.

Applet A program that can be downloaded over a network and launched on the user's computer. See Java.

Archie The system used in searching FTP sites for files. Also Veronica's boyfriend.

ASCII American Standard Code for Information Interchange. A set of 128 alphanumeric and special control characters. ASCII files are also known as plain text files.

AU (.au) a common audio file format for UNIX systems.

AVI Audio/Video Interleaved—a common video file format (.avi). Video quality can be very good at smaller resolutions, but files tend to be rather large.

Bandwidth A measurement of the volume of information that can be transmitted over a network at a given time. Think of a network as a water pipe—the higher the bandwidth (the larger the diameter of the pipe), the more data (water) can pass over the network (through the pipe).

Binary The system by which combinations of 0s and 1s are used to represent any type of data stored on a computer.

Bitmap file   A common image format (.bmp) defined by a rectangular pattern of pixels.

Bookmark   A pointer to a particular Web site. Within browsers, you can bookmark interesting pages so you can return to them easily.

BPS   Bits per second—a measurement of the volume of data that a modem is capable of transmitting. Typical modem speeds today are 14.4 Kbps (14,400 bits per second) and 28.8 Kbps. ISDN offers transfer rates of 128 Kbps.

Browser   A program run on a client computer for viewing World Wide Web pages. Examples include Netscape, Microsoft's Internet Explorer, and Mosaic.

Cache   A region of memory where frequently accessed data can be stored for rapid access.

CGI   Common Gateway Interface—the specification for how an HTTP server should communicate with server gateway applications.

Chat   A system that allows for on-line communication between Internet users. See IRC.

Client   A program (like a Web browser) that connects to and requests information from a server.

Client/server protocol   A communication protocol between networked computers in which the services of one computer (the server) are requested by the other (the client).

Compressed   Data files available for download from the Internet are typically compacted in order to save server space and reduce transfer times. Typical file extensions for compressed files include zip (DOS/Windows) and tar (UNIX).

Cookies   Sweet snacks. Also the collective name for files stored on your hard drive by your Web browser that hold information about your browsing habits, like what sites you have visited, which newsgroups you have read, etc. Many view cookies as an invasion of privacy. To learn about ways to protect your privacy, visit this site for software and information.

Cyberspace*   The computer-created matrix of virtual possibilities, including on-line services, wherein human beings interact with each other and with technology itself.

Dial-up connection   A connection to the Internet via phone and modem. Connection types include PPP and SLIP.

Direct connection   A connection made directly to the Internet—much faster than a dial-up connection.

Discussion group   A particular section within the USENET system typically, though not always, dedicated to a particular subject of interest. Also known as a *newsgroup.*

Domain   The Internet is divided into smaller sets known as domains, including .com (business), .gov (government), .edu (educational), and others.

Domain name   Allows you to reference Internet sites without knowing the true numerical address.

Download   The process of copying data file(s) from a remote computer to a local computer. The opposite action is upload, where a local file is copied to a server.

E-mail   Electronic mail.

Emoticon   A combination of characters that form a facial expression. For example, if you turn your head sideways, the characters :) make a smiley face, and the characters 8) make a four-eyed smiley. Frequently used in e-mail messages to convey a particular tone. If you wanted to jokingly insult somebody, without starting a flame war, you could write, "I think you are a total loser :)".

Eudora   A popular freeware and commercial e-mail management program.

Exchange   Microsoft's integrated fax and e-mail program designed for Windows 95.

FAQ   Frequently Asked Questions—a collection of common questions and answers on a particular subject.

Flame   An insulting message exchanged via e-mail or within newsgroups. A series of flames is known as a *flame war.*

Freeware   Software that is available for download and unlimited use without charge. Compare to shareware.

FTP   File Transfer Protocol—a set of rules for exchanging files between computers via the Internet.

Gateway   Computer hardware and software that allow users to connect from one network to another.

GIF   Graphics Interchange Format—a common image format. Most images seen on Web pages are GIF files.

Gopher   A system allowing users to search for files via menus or directory structures. Uses plain-English names and is text-based only.

Helper application   A program allowing you to view multimedia files that your Web browser cannot handle internally, such as images, audio and video files. The file must be downloaded before it will be displayed/played. Plug-ins allow you to actually view the file over the Internet without downloading first.

Home page   The opening page of a Web site. Also, the Web site that automatically loads each time you launch your browser.

Host   The name of a specific machine within a larger domain.

HOTJAVA   A Web browser developed by Sun Microsystems that takes full advantage of applets written in the Java programming language.

HTML   HyperText Markup Language—a collection of tags typically used in the development of Web pages.

HTTP   HyperText Transfer Protocol—a set of instructions for communication between a server and a World Wide Web client.

Hyperlink   A connection between two anchors. Clicking on one anchor will take you to the linked anchor. Can be within the same document/page or two totally different documents.

HyperText   A document that contains links to other documents, commonly seen in Web pages and help files.

Information superhighway/infobahn   The terms were coined to describe a possible upgrade to the existing Internet through the use of fiber-optic and/or coaxial cable to allow for high-speed data transmission. This highway does not exist—the Internet of today is not an information superhighway.

Internet   The worldwide network of computers communicating via an agreed-upon set of Internet protocols. Odds are that if you are reading this document, you are probably on the Internet right now (just in case you didn't know).

IP address   Internet Protocol address—every computer on the Internet has a unique identifying number, like 209.37.81.17.

IRC   Internet Relay Chat—the system allowing Internet users to conduct online text-based communication with one or more other users.

ISDN   Integrated Services Digital Network—a system of all-digital, high-bandwidth telephone lines allowing for the simultaneous delivery of audio, video, and data. Data travels at 128 Kbps.

ISP   Internet service provider—the company that provides you with a connection to the Internet via either a dial-up connection or a direct connection.

JAVA   A programming language, similar to C, created by Sun Microsystems for developing applets that are capable of running on any computer regardless of the operating system.

JPEG   Joint Photographic Experts Group—a common image format. Most of the images you see embedded into Web pages are GIFs, but sometimes, especially in art or photographic Web sites, you can click on the image to bring up a higher-resolution (larger) JPEG version of the same image.

Kill file   Found within newsreaders, a list of undesirable authors or threads to filter out.

Knowbot   A system for finding Internet user's e-mail addresses via their first and last names. Due to the rapid growth in the volume of e-mail users, this system is not perfect.

LAN   Local area network—a network of computers confined within a small area, such as an office building.

Link   Another name for a hyperlink.

Listserv   An electronic mailing list typically used by a broad range of discussion groups. When you subscribe to a listserv, you will receive periodic e-mail messages about the topic you have requested.

Lurking   The act of reading through mail lists and newsgroups without posting any messages. Considered good netiquette to get the feel of the topic before adding your own two cents.

Lynx   A popular text (nongraphical) World Wide Web Browser.

Mailing list   A list of e-mail addresses to which messages are sent. You can subscribe to a mailing list typically by sending an e-mail to the contact address with the following in the body of the message: the word *subscribe*, the name of the list, and your e-mail address.

Microsoft   C'mon, everybody has heard of Microsoft! Home of Bill Gates. The world's largest operating system and application software development company. Products include Windows 98, NT, XP, the MS Office suite, MS Internet Explorer, and far too many others to list here.

MIDI   Musical Instrument Digital Interface—a high-quality audio file format.

MIME   Multipurpose Internet Mail Extensions, a protocol for allowing e-mail messages to contain various types of media (text, audio, video, images, etc.).

Mirror site   An Internet site set up as an alternative to a busy site; contains copies of all the files stored at the primary location.

Mosaic   One of the first graphical World Wide Web browsers developed at NCSA.

MPEG   Motion Picture Experts Group—a video file format offering excellent quality in a relatively small file. Video files found on the Internet are frequently stored in the MPEG format. Full-length movies (like *Top Gun*) are available on CD and are stored in the MPEG format.

Multimedia   A combination of media types on a single document, including text, graphics, animation, audio, and video.

Name server   A computer running a program that converts domain names into appropriate IP addresses and vice versa.

NCSA   National Center for Supercomputing Applications—an organization headquartered at the University of Illinois. Researchers here created the Mosaic and HTTPD server programs.

Netiquette   Emily Post meets the Internet. Short for Internet etiquette.

Netscape   Netscape used to dominate the market for World Wide Web browsers and servers.

Network   A system of connected computers exchanging information with each other. A LAN is a relatively smaller form of a network in comparison to the Internet, a worldwide network of computers.

Newbie   A new Internet user. If you are reading this definition, you probably are one (or at least were one before you read this).

Newsgroup   A particular section within the USENET system typically, though not always, dedicated to a particular subject of interest. Also known as *discussion groups*.

Newsreader   A program designed for organizing the threads received from a mailing list or newsgroup.

Online   When you connect to the Internet, you are online.

Online service   Services such as America Online, CompuServe, Prodigy, and the Microsoft Network that provide content to subscribers and usually connections to the Internet, though sometimes limited. For instance, online services just recently added Web browsing ability. If you spend a lot of time on the Internet, the fees these services charge add up rapidly.

Packet   A chunk of data. The TCP/IP protocol breaks large data files into smaller "packets" for transmission. When the data reaches its destination, the protocol makes sure that all packets have arrived without error.

Page   An HTML document, or Web site.

PGP   Pretty Good Privacy—an encryption scheme that uses the "public key" approach—messages are encrypted using the publicly available key, but can only be deciphered by the intended recipient via the private key.

Ping   Packet Internet Groper. A program for determining if another computer is presently connected to the Internet.

Pixel   Short for picture element—the smallest unit of resolution on a monitor. Commonly used as a unit of measurement.

PKZIP   A widely available shareware utility allowing users to compress and decompress data files. Helps reduce storage space and transfer times.

Plug-in   A small application that extends the built-in capabilities of your Web browser. Examples include Macromedia's Shockwave, providing animation, and RealAudio, offering streamed sound files over the Internet. Compared to helpers, the multimedia files do not need to be downloaded before shown or played.

POP   Post Office Protocol—a method of storing and returning e-mail.

Post   To send a message to a mailing list or newsgroup.

PPP   Point-to-Point Protocol—a protocol for converting a dial-up connection to a point-to-point connection over the Internet. Frequently used for accessing the World Wide Web over phone lines. Considered more stable than a SLIP connection.

Protocol   An agreed-upon set of rules by which computers exchange information.

Provider   An Internet service provider, or ISP.

Queue   A list of e-mail messages that will be distributed next time you log on to the Internet.

Quicktime   A common video file format created by Apple Computer. Video files found on the Internet are often stored in the QuickTime format—they require a special viewer program for playback.

Register   With shareware, when you contact the vendor and pay for the product, you are registering. In return, you will receive either a password to turn off the nag notices or a copy of the full commercial version.

Robot   A program that automatically searches the World Wide Web for files.

Search engine   A tool for searching for information on the Internet by topic. Popular engines include InfoSeek, Inktomi (Alta Vista), and Web Crawler.

Server   One-half of the client/server protocol, runs on a networked computer and responds to requests submitted by the client. Your World Wide Web browser is a client of a World Wide Web server.

SGML   Standard General Markup Language—a standard for markup languages. HTML is one version of SGML.

Shareware   Software that is available on a free, limited-trial basis. Sometimes this is a fully featured product; other times it lacks some of the features of the commercial version. If you find the product useful, you are expected to register the software, for which in return you will receive the full-featured commercial version.

Signature   A personal tag automatically appended to an e-mail message. May be short, such as the author's name, or quite long, such as a favorite quote.

Site   A single Web page or a collection of related Web pages.

SLIP   Serial Line Internet Protocol—a protocol allowing you to use a dial-up connection as an Internet connection. Similar to a PPP connection, though far less stable.

SMTP   Simple Mail Transfer Protocol—a protocol dictating how e-mail messages are exchanged over the Internet.

Snail mail   Plain old paper mail. United States Post Office. Cliff Claven delivered snail mail when he wasn't drinking with Norm at Cheers.

SPAM   *Non-Internet:* Delicious "meat" in a can! *Internet:* Sending multiple, sometimes thousands, of unwelcome messages to a newsgroup or mailing list to promote a commercial product or Web site.

Subscribe   To become a member of. One can subscribe to a mailing list, a newsgroup, an on-line service, or an Internet service.

T1   A category of leased telephone line service allowing transfer rates of 1.5 Mbps (megabytes per second) over the Internet. Too expensive for home users (around $2,000 per month), but commonly found in business environments.

TAR   Tape archive—a compression format commonly used in the transfer and storage of files residing on UNIX computers.

TCP/IP   Transmission Control Protocol/Internet Protocol—this protocol is the foundation of the Internet, an agreed-upon set of rules directing computers on how to exchange information with each other. Other Internet protocols, such as FTP, Gopher, and HTTP, sit on top of TCP/IP.

Telnet   A protocol for logging on to remote computers from anywhere on the Internet.

Thread   An ongoing message-based conversation on a single subject.

TIFF   Tagged Image File Format—a popular graphic image file format.

Trolling   Deliberately posting false information in order to elicit responses from people who really want to help. A typical response might be, "No, Bart Simpson was NOT one of our founding fathers."

UNIX   A powerful operating system used on the backbone machines of the Internet. World Wide Web servers frequently run on UNIX.

Upload   To copy a file from a local computer connected to the Internet to a remote computer. Opposite is download.

URL   Uniform Resource Locator—the method by which Internet sites are addressed. An example would be "http://www.squareone.com," the address of the Square One home page.

Usenet   Short for user's network. The collection of the thousands of bulletin boards residing on the Internet. Each bulletin board contains discussion groups, or newsgroups, dedicated to a myriad of topics. Messages are posted and responded to by readers either as public or private e-mails.

Veronica   The system used in searching Gopher menus for topics. Also Archie's girlfriend.

Virus*   A malicious and generally quite small software program designed and written to adversely affect your computer by altering the way it works without your knowledge or permission.

Visit Synonymous with viewing a World Wide Web site.

WAIS Wide Area Information Server—a system of searchable text databases.

WAN Wide area network—a system of connected computers spanning a large geographical area.

WAV Waveform audio (.wav)—a common audio file format for DOS/Windows computers.

Winsock A Microsoft Windows DLL file that provides the interface to TCP/IP services, essentially allowing Windows to use Web browsers, FTP programs, and others.

WWW World Wide Web, or simply Web. A subset of the Internet which uses a combination of text, graphics, audio, and video (multimedia) to provide information on almost every subject imaginable.

X Bitmap An uncompressed black-and-white-image file format (.xbm).

X Pixelmap An uncompressed color-image file format (.xpm).

XML* Extensible markup language—an emerging Web standard.

Yahoo! A Web directory created by a couple of guys from Stanford who now have more money than the entire state of Arkansas. Rumor has it they own one business suit between them. Their site is constantly updated and provides an easy way of finding almost any Web page. Check it out for yourself at www.yahoo.com.

ZIP A compressed file format (.zip). Many files available on the Internet are compressed or zipped in order to reduce storage space and transfer times. To uncompress the file, you need a utility like PKZIP (DOS) or WinZip (Windows).

Endnotes

1. Adam Gaffin, *The Electronic Frontier Foundation's Guide to the Internet*, Version 3.20 (December 11, 1996).
2. Michael Hanrahan, "History of the Internet," Web posted at http://www.wayoutthere.com/idrc/history/index.html.
3. Tracy LaQuey and Jeanne C. Ryer, *The Internet Companion: A Beginner's Guide to Global Networking* (Reading, MA: Addison-Wesley, 1993), on-line version.
4. Gregory R. Gromov, "History of Internet and WWW: The Roads and Crossroads of Internet's History," Web posted at: http://www.internetvalley.com/intval.html.
5. Many of the definitions in this manual are adapted from SquareOne Technology's *Internet Glossary*, which is reprinted as a glossary in this book.
6. Not all host computers use registered domain names. The number of registered domain names reached 30 million in October 2000, and is expected to exceed 75 million by early 2002.
7. The Internet Industry Almanac projects 601 million worldwide Internet users by 2002. See "U.S. Leads in Number of Internet Users," *Silicon Valley/San Jose Business Journal*, October 30, 2000. Web posted at http://sanjose.bcentral.com/sanjose/stories/2000/10/30/daily11.html. Accessed February 6, 2001. An Internet user is defined by the publication as any person over 16 who uses the Internet on a regular basis at least once a month.
8. "Technology," Clinton Campaign Position Paper, September 16, 1992.
9. The assignment of IP addresses is made through a central Internet Registry, which is separate from the InterNIC.
10. Tim Berners-Lee, and Robert Cailliau. "WorldWideWeb: Proposal for a HyperText Project," p. 2. Undated. Web posted at http://www.w3.org/pub/WWW/Proposal. (According to Robert Cailliau's "A Little History of the World Wide Web," October 3, 1995—Web posted at http://www.w3.org/pub/WWW/History.html—the proposal was submitted in October 1990.)
11. February 1996 issue.
12. SquareOne Technology, "How Do I Locate and Use a Helper Application?" Web posted at http://www.squareonetech.com/helper.html.
13. Cecil Greek, "Using the Internet as a Newsmaking Criminology Tool." Presentation given at the American Society of Criminology annual meeting, San Diego, CA, November 20, 1997. Web posted at http://www.fsu.edu/~crimdo/asc-sd.htm.

14. Bob Shinmachi, "You Must Manage Your E-Mail," *Planet IT*. Web posted at http://www.planetit.com/techcenters/docs/enterprise_apps_systems-storage/opinion/ PIT20000118S0023. Accessed February 22, 2001.

15. Internet telephony, or the use of Internet services to carry voice communications, is still in its infancy. In the not-too-distant future, however, many people will be able to talk over the Internet in much the same way that they send e-mail or participate in chat rooms today.

16. *Essays*, bk. 3, ch. 9, "Of Vanity" (1588).

17. We should say "easily available," since messages are routinely stored on listservers for a period of time and *can* be accessed by anyone with sufficient expertise at issuing listserv commands. Most, however, would not regard the process as easy.

18. See the Leathernet.Com Glossary at http://www.learnthenet.com/english/glossary/glossary.htm.

19. Cyveillance, "Internet Exceeds 2 Billion Pages: Cyveillance Study Projects Internet Will Double in Size by Early 2001." Web posted at http://www.cyveillance.com/us/newsroom/pressr/000710.asp. Accessed March 10, 2001.

20. The National Criminal Justice Reference Service Abstracts Database Help Page. http://excalib1.aspensys.com/rware/help.html. Accessed March 10, 2001.

21. Northern Light search tips. Web posted at http://northernlight.com/docs/search_help_ optimize.html. Accessed March 10, 2001.

22. Visit CPSR at http://www.cpsr.org.

23. The Computer Ethics Institute may be reached at Computer Ethics Institute, 11 Dupont Circle, NW, Suite 900, Washington, DC 20036.

24. From the classic guide by Arlene Rinaldi, *The Net: User Guidelines and Netiquette*, Web posted at http://www.fau.edu/rinaldi/net/ten.html.

25. See Albion.com's netiquette section at http://www.albion.com/netiquette/index.html.

26. *Twenty-Four Hours*, 15 Dec. 1969, BBC-TV. From *The Columbia Dictionary of Quotations*. Copyright © 1993 by Columbia University Press.

27. C. Northcote Parkinson, *The Pursuit of Progress* (London: John Murray 1958).

28. Information derived and partially quoted from govtjobs.com. Web posted at http://www.govtjobs.com/index.html. Accessed March 5, 2001.

29. Taken from http://www.fbi.gov/employment/agent2.htm. Accessed March 10, 2001.

30. Cynthia Mason and Charles Ardai, *Future Crime: An Anthology of the Shape of Crime to Come* (New York: Donald I. Fine, 1992), p. xiii.

31. The company that created the RSA standard is RSA Data Security, Inc. It is based in Redwood City, California, and can be reached at (415) 595-8782 or at http://www.rsa.com.

32. See the CERT® home page, http://www.cert.org.

33. Definition adapted from Norton AntiVirus Web site. See http://www.norton.com.

34. While there are sometimes ways to recover from these kinds of viral attacks, they are best left to professionals.

Index